Praise for Monica Loughman's Dancing

'Monica Loughman and Alan Foley as the doomed lovers created a world of mystery and romance which captivated the imagination of the audience completely.'

Jo Kerrigan, *The Irish Examiner*

'The role of Odette demands stratified characterisation, from initial fear to love and idealism, and Monica Loughman allows the changes to subtly pass through her. She never veers towards melodrama, but captures just the right blend of dignity, vulnerability and poise.'

Michael Seaver, *The Irish Times*

'Giselle is required to express depths of pain and love, which Loughman captures eloquently. By dancing with him until daybreak she saves his life; this exquisite pas de deux, in which the disembodied Giselle seems to slip through Albrecht's arms, gliding en pointe, transforms the problematic notion of female sacrifice into a more universal expression of forgiveness and transcendence.'

Helen Meany, *The Irish Times*

'Alone on stage Monica Loughman danced the Dying Swan . . . with a quiet presence and confident technique.'

Michael Seaver, *The Irish Times*

'This fledgling 20-year-old ballerina imbued her role with a fragility and sweetness that captured the heart, while Alan Foley as her partner was a strong, supportive and deeply caring Prince Siegfried catching her gently as she fell softly backwards like a stemmed flower . . . can we see more ballet miracles like Monica?'

Maureen Kelleher, *The Irish Examiner*

'She made a lovely Odette . . . her superb grace and technique, made everything she did look easy.'

Carolyn Swift, *The Irish Times*

'Artist to watch: Dubliner Monica Loughman, who joined the corps de ballet of the Perm State Opera And Ballet Company on completion of her training at the Perm Academy and is being groomed for stardom.'

Carolyn Swift, *The Irish Times*

Ballerina

Monica Loughman

with

Jean Harrington

BOOK REPUBLIC

A BOUTIQUE PUBLISHING PRESS

First published in Ireland in 2004 by Maverick House
Publishers,
Office 19, Dunboyne Business Park, Dunboyne, Co.
Meath, Ireland

This edition printed in November 2011 by Book Republic,
an imprint of Maverick House Publishers.

www.bookrepublic.ie
email: info@bookrepublic.ie

ISBN 978-1-907221-23-1

10 9 8 7 6 5 4 3

The paper used in this book comes from wood pulp of
managed forests. For every tree felled, at least one tree is
planted, thereby renewing natural resources.

A CIP catalogue record for this book is available from the
British Library.

*This book is dedicated to Damien, Dad and Siobhán,
and is in memory of Monica (Mammy) Loughman,
and my big sister Eileen Loughman*

Foreword

So many things have changed and so much has happened since I first wrote this book. I hardly recognize the voice behind the story, all the facts are there but I have changed in so many ways. My sister Eileen passed away of pancreatic cancer just two months before I had my little boy, Damien. Now that I am a mum myself and I work so much with young people I can see why people were so taken by this story, if only because so much happened at such a young age. Only now do I finally feel that Ireland is my home, thanks to Damien, and I have and continue to work hard to find my place in a society that has no special place for ballet. Sometimes I miss my Russian home and the buzz of the theatre, the smell and the sounds, but I do not miss the politics.

Over the past five years I have been working hard on my own ballet schools and company which began life as the Irish Youth Russian Ballet, but since all the girls have grown in skill as well as years it has transformed into the Monica Loughman Ballet Company. I want to bring full scale ballet productions to Ireland with all Irish ballerinas, the only difference is they can stay in Ireland and receive Russian training from me and the guest teachers from Russia, among other places. The company started life with 16 girls dancing The Snowflakes from The Nutcracker. Now it boasts almost 70 dancers, both male and female. I hope that one day Ireland can find a place for its own full time professional ballet company and that our young people will never have to leave home to follow their dreams…

—Monica Loughman (October, 2011)

Acknowledgements

I'd like to thank my family, who have supported me through good times and bad.

My Dad's constant question, 'Are you okay for money?' is his way of offering support and showing me how much he cares.

His love means so much to me. I know he's always looking out for me and I love him for it, and for other reasons too many to mention.

Siobhán and Eileen have been a great support to me, keeping my feet firmly on the ground, in a way that only sisters can.

My niece Niamh, otherwise known as Nini, fills my heart with joy and has inspired new emotions in me. She even makes me smile at six o'clock in the morning.

My heartfelt thanks go to all the Irish students who shared my adventures and misadventures in Perm; what wonderful memories we possess from those days.

I would like to thank Alan Foley for being my friend, my dancing partner, and my boss. I owe him a debt of gratitude for all his help, advice, and support with this book.

Bal'shoy spasiba to Valintina Bykova, my teacher, who made me believe in myself and in her. Her reliable tuition reminded me that dancing is a pleasure, despite the hardships that sometimes surround it. I hope to someday influence people in the way that she does.

Rimma Siraeva's sense of enthusiasm infected me; she's a joy to be around, never failing to amaze me with her outlandish ideas.

Spasiba—to all my colleagues, friends and teachers in Perm State Ballet, for making me feel so at home in Russia. The foothills of the Ural Mountains are now my second home because of the love and warmth you have shown me.

Regina Rogers gave me the support I desperately needed when I was dancing at a time when my mother was terminally ill. I will always be grateful for your kindness.

Thanks to my first ballet teacher, Marie Cole, for planting the seeds that led to my career.

I'm also very grateful to John Baraldi for opening the world of Russian ballet to me.

Because of all the problems with the various artistic directors, I never expected to be put forward for solo or principal roles, and when it happened I greatly appreciated it.

Although I didn't always see eye to eye with them, I always respected the difficult job they had in trying to keep everyone happy.

Although my fellow student Donna Addie and I sometimes fought like cats and dogs in the early years, she's been my best friend and true supporter for many years, and I thank her for that.

Jimmy, Sally and James Dunne are the gentlest and nicest people I have ever met. Thanks to Rosita Wolfe for giving me words of advice when I needed them most. Damien O'Neill; thanks for seeing the potential in me.

A big thank you to the late Carolyn Swift, who was my first supporter and whom I will always fondly remember. A huge thanks to Jean Harrington, who sifted through months of my gibberish, and without whom this book would never have happened. Thank you for making this project work.

And finally, thanks to my Mam. No words can describe how much I miss you and how much I love you.

—Monica Loughman (2004)

To Monica Loughman who turned me into a balletomane, and who made writing this so much fun —thank you! I learnt so much about Russia and ballet during our many hours of conversation.

To my friends: Jackie Conlon, Gillian Galvin, Corina Bradley, Orlagh Leonard, Caitríona McCarthy and Catherine O'Reilly—one of you is always around when I need you. Thanks for everything.

A huge thanks to Alan Foley and Susan Harrington who edited the manuscript so carefully. Their comments were much appreciated. I'm also grateful to Regina Rogers for all her assistance.

Thanks to my mother, Aveen, who has always supported me throughout my career, and in my life. You are my inspiration. To my father who always believed in me; despite the passage of time, I still miss you in my life.

I'm lucky that my family are also my friends; my sisters Susie and Ann—I'd be lost without you. My brothers Robert and Martin—you are like night and day. Life wouldn't make sense without you both in it.

Thanks to my beloved Aoileann and Oisín for changing my life, and showing me a wonderful world I knew nothing about. Finally to their dad, John for changing my world; I'll always be grateful.

—Jean Harrington (October 2011)

Chapter One

Sometimes I find it hard to believe that my story is unique. It's true that a small number of Irish girls studied ballet in Russia, but my story differs from theirs because I was the first Western European to join the Perm State Theatre of Opera and Ballet. I am the one they call 'The Irish Ballerina'.

I'll start at the beginning of the tale, though it may appear at first that I am starting halfway through my life.

I started ballet when I was four years old, however, it was in Russia that I became the dancer I am today. My path to becoming a professional began when I was accepted to the Russian State Choreographic Institute of Ballet in Perm.

I was taking classes at the Marie Cole School of Ballet in Dublin when I heard about auditions for the school in Perm. I knew immediately I wanted to go because it was the opportunity of a lifetime. Russian ballerinas and dancers had always enthralled me. The prospect of studying under a Russian ballet master had always seemed unattainable, but fate intervened and I was offered this unique chance.

I told my parents I wanted to audition. They were very supportive but asked if ballet was a career I genuinely wanted to pursue. I don't think they really believed that I would be accepted, and they figured they would cross that bridge if, and when, the time came.

I turned up to the audition at Digges Lane Studio in Dublin city full of nerves. I didn't know what to expect. When I entered the corridor, it was thronged with girls in leg-warmers, stretching and chatting. They seemed infinitely more experienced than I was, and I looked in horror as they did moves I just couldn't do. There were so many people waiting that we were split into three groups.

I was put into the second group and I waited impatiently until we were ushered into the classroom. I took my position at the side of the room and we were introduced to Madame Sakharova.

She was the principal and artistic director of the Perm school and was highly esteemed in the ballet world. She had been a soloist in the Bolshoi Ballet before becoming a soloist and later a teacher in Perm. One of her most famous students was Nadezhda Pavlova, who at 16 years of age was the youngest person to win the Grand Prize at the 1973 Moscow International Ballet Competition. Pavlova instantly became a prima ballerina.

I was only 13-years-old and I couldn't believe this legendary teacher was standing in front of me. I was almost afraid to dance for her and I nervously awaited the class. She struck me as an authoritative woman. She welcomed us briefly and asked us to take our places at the barre. I had never danced in a proper studio with mirrors and barres before and I found it intimidating to see my reflection in the glass.

As she took us through a variety of simple movements that included pliés and tendues, it became apparent that she was looking for potential rather than assessing our current technique. She walked around the room and poked and prodded us during the class. During a ronde de jambe combination she suddenly grabbed my leg and brought it up to my head.

I struggled to maintain my composure and let her twist my leg around without blinking, although I was sure she could sense my pain.

At the end of the class the third group did the same routines while we waited nervously outside. When they finished, Madame Sakharova hung a list on the corridor wall, which contained the names of the successful applicants. To my disbelief and delight, I had been accepted. I jumped around the hall in excitement, hugging my mother and my friend, Nicola McCarthy, who had also passed the audition. Madame Sakharova next called the selected dancers back into the studio where she congratulated us.

'Well done! You are the lucky ones that will be coming to our wonderful school next year.'

She walked up to Nicola and I and looked at us in puzzlement. 'You are so young,' she said, in a thick Russian accent. 'You'll miss your home? No?'

We assured her that we were more than willing to leave, and I silently pleaded with my eyes. I wanted this more than anything. She looked at us for a minute and then seemed to make up her mind. She smiled, placed her hand on my back and said, 'Okay then. You are welcome.'

I responded with a huge smile and she turned on her heels and left.

It was August 1992 and I had just turned 14 when I stepped off the plane at Moscow's international airport, Sheremetyevo-2. My long, brown hair was swept up in a ponytail, and under my jacket I wore my favourite purple jumper which was adorned with teddy bears. My immediate concern was that of my luggage: I had brought 60kgs worth of books, clothes, toilet rolls, cosmetics, and food in one suitcase. I also carried another bag weighing 20kgs on my back. It meant that I took my first steps through Russia looking like a crippled old woman, rather than a graceful, young ballet dancer.

We dragged our luggage to the minibus that was waiting to bring us to our accommodation. The driver tossed the luggage into the boot and we headed off to our lodgings for the night.

There were 13 of us altogether and we were escorted by John Baraldi of the Irish International Cultural Education Trust. He acted as our chaperone.

John had a passion for ballet and a real interest in promoting it in Ireland. He had actually helped arrange the auditions and set up the study programme. I liked John instantly and trusted his ability to sort out any problems or misunderstandings that might occur. He was very laid back but he could lose his cool quickly if necessary.

He was a tall man who always wore a beige trench coat and smoked incessantly. Before we left Dublin, he told us that he would look after us no matter what happened and we believed him without question. He had a calming influence on people and was placid in most situations.

He knew how excited we were at being in Russia and organised for us to stay overnight in Moscow. The minibus took us to our accommodation which was a stately home on the outskirts of the city.

It was spectacular and evoked romantic images of Moscow at its finest. The building had steps up to the front door, with pillars on both sides and windows from floor to ceiling either side of the main entrance. We were shown to our room, which was laid out in a dormitory style.

The girls piled into the bedroom where we dumped our luggage. James Dunne from Cabra in Dublin was the only boy on the trip, so he had a room to himself. The building was being used as an artists' retreat, and it's interior's faded elegance reminded me of an old ballerina who still wore her long, grey hair in a bun, and continued to wear her tutus long after she could perform. I was fascinated by my surroundings and wandered through the manor long after the other girls had tired of it.

The following morning John brought us on a tour around Moscow. It was a city unlike any other I had seen. There were trams on the roads and the buildings were wider and taller than those in Dublin. Although it was a sunny morning, all the Russians wore heavy coats in muted blacks and browns, made from natural fabrics. We stood out instantly as typical Westerners. We wore jumpers and jeans, with coloured synthetic jackets. The Muscovites looked at us as if we had landed from the moon.

The language was the first thing to throw me. I had been lucky enough to enjoy foreign holidays with my family, and had picked up a few French and Spanish words on my travels. I thought I might recognise the structure of some Russian words, but I couldn't have been more wrong. It was completely different to anything I had ever heard. Even a simple 'yes' (*da*) sounded curious.

After a brief visit to Red Square and some lunch, we boarded the 'Kama' train to Perm, which was named after the river that flows through Perm. When we boarded the 'Kama', I dragged my suitcase into a compartment with my friend Nicola following close behind. Two girls named Donna Addie and Claire Rooney joined us and we tried to make ourselves comfortable for the long journey ahead.

The cabin was about the size of an average bathroom, so you can imagine how squashed it was with our six months of provisions. Meanwhile other students were also squashing their luggage into cabins next to us. There was four to each cabin. The first one housed Emma O'Kane, Caitriona Lowry, Ella Clark and Anna Moore. Katherine O'Malley, Catherine Loane, Nicola Jane Mullan, and Claire Keating were next to them. John and James took the cabin adjacent to theirs.

As the train chugged across the Russian countryside, I felt I was part of something historical; something wonderful. Butterflies kept fluttering in my tummy, but I pushed them away assuring myself that everything would be fine. It wasn't quite dusk and there was a warm, red glow in the sky. I watched the shadowy trees hurtle by and daydreamed about what lay ahead. I started chatting to my companions, knowing they would be the closest link to home for the next few months.

Donna was from Raheny in Dublin, which was near my home in Santry, and at 15, she was a year and a half older than me. She had an athletic build, and a healthy glow, which made her look like a classical ballerina. We struck up an instant rapport. In fact, this was the beginning of a life-long friendship.

Very soon there was a party atmosphere on board the train. Girls were running between the cabins telling stories and jokes and sharing their sweets. John Baraldi popped his head into our cabin every now and then to make sure we were okay. As it grew late, we made up our bunk beds and I changed into my pajamas. I was on the top bunk opposite Nicola while Donna and Claire were in the bottom bunks.

I tried to sleep, as I knew it would take 22 hours to get to Perm. Whenever I am anxious or excited —and on this journey I was both— my sleeping pattern is the first thing to be affected. By 11 o'clock, however, even I had succumbed to slumber, lulled by the rhythmic chugga chugga of the 'Kama'.

The train trundled into the city of Perm the next afternoon. All the girls were clambering for window space to get their first glimpse of the city that was to be our home for the next few years. I felt a shiver of excitement pulsate to the pit of my stomach. I couldn't believe that I was finally going to study ballet in this classical school.

The platform was crowded with blonde-haired Russian boys jostling for space and waving at us. Some of them jumped onto the train and started pulling our luggage onto the platform and onto trolleys that were lined up. I dragged my suitcase along the train corridor where a good-looking boy took it from me and lifted it into his arms. His knees buckled for a split second before he steadied himself again. I blushed immediately. He started talking to me in Russian but I couldn't understand what he was trying to say. I could tell from the puzzled expression on his face, though, that he was trying to work out what I had in my case. It weighed more than I did.

Two of the girls had studied in Perm the previous year, Katherine and Catherine, and they started hugging some of the boys, and talking to them in halted Russian. I just stood on the platform for a minute watching the light of the August sun dance through the trees, and listening to the melodious, strange dialect that surrounded me.

I saw a woman in her 40s with short, brown, curly hair embrace John like a long lost friend. This was Elena, who would become our Russian language teacher.

She wore rimmed glasses and had a lovely, welcoming smile. I recognised her immediately from a television documentary about the ballet school that had been screened shortly after our auditions. I immediately warmed to her and to the atmosphere of the school. The Russian boys were very chivalrous and made a point of carrying our bags.

We were directed to a minibus that looked like a loaf of bread on four wheels. It was perfectly square and looked nothing like the green buses of Dublin.

The journey to the ballet school took 10 minutes. It was at this point that I suddenly realised there was no going back. If I felt lonely or homesick, it wasn't a matter of a quick trip home. I was going to live in this foreign country on my own, and try to become a ballerina. The further the bus travelled, the more alone I felt. The anxiety took a hold of my stomach and twisted it hard. It started to rise inside me, but I swallowed it back down vigorously.

Calm down, Monica! You'll be fine, I told myself over and over. I started talking to Katherine and she distracted me by talking about our living quarters.

As we turned a corner, the school appeared as if from nowhere. It was an imposing, mustard-coloured building, three stories high. There was a collective gasp as we realised the significance of our arrival. I was overwhelmed.

I couldn't believe that I had made it to Russia to train as a ballerina. Finally I was standing on the brink of my dream.

Chapter Two

In World War II the Kirov Ballet, together with the opera, orchestra, and training schools, evacuated to Perm from St. Petersburg.

This temporary arrangement stretched to three years and during this time, Perm became the artistic heart of the Soviet Union. When the blockade was raised in 1944, the Kirov theatre and school went home, but some of the dancers and teachers from the Maryinsky Troupe stayed to found the Perm State Ballet School and Theatre.

However, the Perm theatre always maintained close links with the Kirov and many of the students from Perm joined the Kirov upon graduation. The lyrical style taught in the school is directly inherited from the Kirov.

The Perm State Theatre of Opera and Ballet is located very close to the school and has a long classical history, with its own opera company, ballet company and orchestra under the same roof. The theatre itself was built in 1870.

The building where we were to live for the next few years was called the Internat. It lay directly across the road from the school and was painted the same colour.

The Internat was five storeys high and had five or six steps leading to a porch, with about 12 windows looking out on the front.

'Stay with the bags,' I shouted to Nicola, as I ran up the steps into the foyer. Katherine had told me that it was a case of first come, first served in reserving the bedrooms, so I knew I had to get there quickly. There were two staircases in the foyer, one leading up the right side and one on the left. I raced up the right-hand staircase and didn't stop running until I got to the fifth floor. I ran down to the end of the hall where I saw a double room. I sat down on one of the beds and waited patiently for Nicola to arrive with her bags. A few of the older girls came into my room and tried to take the room from me but I wouldn't give in. It was complete chaos. One of the girls took a while to find an empty bed, so she kept dragging her suitcase from room to room.

I took in my surroundings while I waited on Nicola. The room was clean but very basic. The walls were covered with pink floral wallpaper and pale pink curtains hung from the windows. There were two single steel beds with very thin mattresses. The mattresses were awful—they were covered with stains and looked dreadful. The school provided us with blankets and sheets, and after we had lodged all of our belongings in our room, we set about making up our beds. Everyone got a white sheet and a red blanket with a duvet cover. My duvet cover had a big circular hole in the middle. I thought that someone had peed on it, and had cut out the centre to save embarrassment.

'Nicola, look. I think someone made a hole in my duvet cover.'

'Yes! That's very strange, isn't it? Why would someone do that?' Nicola replied.

She set about making her bed and soon realised that her duvet cover had the same hole as mine.

'Mine is the same! That's odd. I wonder are they all like this or was there a systematic bed-wetter here last year?' We both looked at each other and laughed. We soon realised this was just one of the small, but many differences between life in Perm and Dublin.

When we had made our beds, Elena came up and brought us over to the ballet school to have something to eat. We walked across giggling and chatting. We couldn't believe there was a tram line so close to the school. It was fascinating. We went straight to the canteen on the ground floor where we were told it was time for *poldnik*.

Poldnik is what the Russians call a snack—they usually have a snack between lunch and dinner, and today, they were having *smetana* and tea. *Smetana* is like Greek yogurt but with sugar in it. It's sweet, and I found it very sickly.

The tea looked like dirty brown water, as if someone had boiled their sock in it and poured it onto a layer of sugar. It was horrible. I ate less than a spoonful of *smetana* and took a sip from the tea. It was then I realised that I would rather starve than eat the food on offer.

The *smetana* was accompanied by a slice of rock hard bread, and I feared I might lose a tooth if I tried to bite it.

I couldn't believe how dreadful the food was. I thought I would never get used to it, however, over the years I gradually grew to love *smetana*, as indeed, I came to love most Russian cuisine. At that moment in time, though, it made me retch.

After we finished *poldnik*, Elena brought us to see our classroom, which was on the third floor of the school. We were brought up a huge square-shaped staircase, which only went up as far as the second floor. We then walked down a narrow corridor with squeaky wooden floors, past the Russian students changing rooms. This led to another set of smaller stairs that went directly up to our Russian language classroom, which doubled as our changing room.

Our ballet classroom was quite small, but it was better than anything I had danced in at home. On one side of the room there were large windows; on the opposite side there were ceiling to floor mirrors, with a bench for the teacher to sit on. An upright piano stood in one corner. The wooden floor was worn at the barre, where hundreds of students had practised over the years.

There were six other large ballet classrooms on this floor. The room next door was identical to ours only it was bigger. This was where the Russians took their class. Elena continued to show us around the school.

The building enchanted me. There were three classrooms on the first floor with study rooms and the assistant director's office. The ground floor housed the canteen and six piano rooms. The academic classrooms were also situated here.

During the tour, we came upon a ballet class where the students were doing simple but fabulous moves. We sat and watched them. They had such a clean style it was a joy to watch. They were toned and flexible and only looked about 11 years of age.

I started to worry because I wondered how I was ever going to reach their standard, considering they were so good at such a young age.

When the class finished, Elena told us that these students were the same age as us, so the gap wasn't as big as I'd initially feared. She then brought us back down to the canteen for dinner. As we approached the doors I could hear the familiar chatter of students, but when we walked inside, the canteen went silent as the students stared at us.

Most of the girls had their hair in buns and wore leotards with legwarmers and ballet shoes. I thought that I had stepped into another world. I couldn't wait to get into that gear. It was so exciting. They looked as if they knew exactly what they were doing.

But the Russian students looked at us with disdain. I looked at my doc marten boots and jeans and felt clumsy and awkward beside their elegance. After about three seconds of silence, the crowd resumed their chat and we picked up trays and queued to receive our first Russian dinner. The dinner ladies on the other side of the counter weren't very friendly as they handed out plates of cabbage and burgers. The burgers looked like big lumps of meat drizzled in their own juices; they were thoroughly unappetising therefore I could only eat the cabbage.

Elena told us to be in ballet class at ten thirty the next morning and left us to relax in our rooms for the evening. Nicola and I unpacked our cases and tried to make the room a little bit homely. I had brought over a stereo so we tried to find a Russian radio station that played modern music. But there was none, so we just listened to some Eastern European pop.

Eventually we grew tired and went to bed but I couldn't sleep. I tried to absorb all that had happened over the last two days. I felt a mixture of emotions.

I could feel the competition around me; it made the hairs on the back of my neck tingle. I was nervous and this made me nauseous.

Nicola fell into a slumber instantly but, try as I might, I just couldn't go to sleep. I knew it was going to be a really tough year. I was so afraid that I'd go into class the next morning and the teacher would think I wasn't good enough. I put myself under so much pressure that I wound myself into a state of high anxiety.

I was quite religious and had taken a Novena prayer book with me to Russia. I took this from my locker, and brought it into the hall with my torch. The hall widened in the middle and there was a couch pushed up against the wall. While the rest of the students slept, I sat on the couch and prayed to the Sacred Heart to grant me all my heart's desires. I prayed for my family in Ireland and for my success in this strange and new environment. The more I thought about home, the lonelier I felt and when I finished praying I put the Novena on the couch beside the torch and cried my eyes out. I cried until I could cry no more and I was utterly exhausted, so I went back to my room, climbed into my lumpy bed and slept.

The following morning I got dressed in a leotard, and I put my hair in a bun. When I looked in the mirror,

I realised how bulky and thick it was compared to the Russian girls who wore paper thin buns. Nicola was ready and told me to hurry up, and get over to the classroom.

'Look at the state of this bun, Nicola!' I exclaimed. 'It looks as if I've got a muffin tied to my head. How do the Russians make theirs so thin? Did you notice how their whole profile is slimmer because of it?'

'Not really,' Nicola sighed. 'Come on, we'll be late. You can fix your hair later.'

'No, I'm going to do it again, and try to get it right. I'll be over in a few minutes.'

Nicola left and I redid my bun, but without much success. It looked as bulky as the first time. It later became an obsession of ours to get our buns as slim as the Russians. Donna was able to do hers perfectly so I was always pestering her to show me how to do it.

After a few more minutes playing with my hair, I made my way over to our ballet classroom. When I got there, Nicola was already warming up with Anna and Emma. I threw my tracksuit in a corner and joined Nicola at the barre. She had positioned herself in the middle of the back barre facing the mirror. This was the best spot in the classroom because you could see yourself in the mirror and correct yourself as you danced. I was disgusted that I hadn't gotten there first to get the prime spot, but a thought suddenly occurred to me.

'Can I stand beside you, Nicola?'

'Of course! Squeeze in there.'

'Would you like to rotate positions every other day so I could get a look in the mirror?'

'Sure, why not,' Nicola replied, and went back to her stretches.

I couldn't believe she had agreed to rotate with me. I was delighted because I would have been left at the edge for the rest of the year, if not. Caitriona, Donna, Nicola Jane and Claire took their positions on the side barres.

After a few minutes a tiny, blonde woman swept into the room. 'Hello *devochky!*' she said with a big smile. She wore glasses that seemed too big for her delicate face and she walked quickly and neatly.

She had already exhausted her English vocabulary so she continued in Russian. Pointing at herself she said, 'Svetlana.' She proceeded to walk around the room and point at each girl individually to ascertain our names. She tried to find out how old we were, but with our lack of Russian and her lack of English, it was a long, drawn-out affair.

After about 30 minutes, she picked up a plastic watering can from the corner of the room and sprinkled water at our feet. She tried to explain, in a mixture of sign language and Russian, that it would add resistance to the floor and prevent us from slipping. With that, she began our first class.

She stood at the barre, flicked off her shoe and started doing tendues. The bones of her feet were deformed, but they were still pointed beautifully.

Anyone who has a cursory knowledge of ballet will know that a tendue is one of the most basic moves, so I thought she was doing a quick run through the basics, before teaching us more complicated steps.

Svetlana walked around the classroom and moved our legs into the positions she wanted. When she came to me, she dug her hands deep into my shoulder blades to make me stand straighter and taller. She moved my thigh until she was satisfied it looked correct and then moved on to the next girl. I looked at myself in the mirror and saw a subtle change in my profile. I looked more elegant and graceful but I felt as awkward as ever. We stayed on the barre doing tendues for the entire class, but I hoped we would start dancing the following day. I have to say I was disappointed at the end of the class; I didn't travel this far to practise positions I was already bored with.

We spent the entire first week, however, on the barre doing tendues and pliés over and over again. It seemed to take forever to co-ordinate our leg and arm movements to her exacting standards. We had been trained completely differently, and the language barrier guaranteed everything took twice as long.

Pretty soon it became apparent that Svetlana had a habit of adopting favourites in the class and Donna was the first to attain this lucky position. Donna was tall and had very long legs with a tiny body. When she lifted her leg, it went over her head without much effort. The only thing that went against Donna was that she carried a bit of extra weight and it seemed to gather around her midriff and bum. This would later cause her major problems in the school. But Svetlana was in love with her and went around the room crying 'Don-na! Don-na!' every time she got something right.

During this time, she ignored the rest of the class and acted as if there was no one else in the room. But she switched her attentions very quickly. Almost as soon as she got excited about someone, she would drop her. It was very tough on the people that were being ignored. It created a terrible undercurrent of jealousy, although I'm sure it was a very clever and calculated move on her behalf.

I hated being ignored and I tried desperately to do the moves in the manner in which she wanted, but it was extremely difficult because I didn't quite know what she was looking for. After a few days of watching her work with Donna and some of the other girls, I went to Katherine in frustration to see if she could shed any light on what Svetlana wanted from us.

Katherine was in Sakharova's class with Ella, Catherine and a number of Russian girls. I looked up to these girls and valued their opinion. I waited for Katherine after class one day and went into the classroom as she was putting on her tracksuit.

'Oh hi, Monica. How are you settling into the school?'

'Okay, but I was wondering if you could help me with something. Svetlana has spent about five days doing tendues with us, and I don't really understand what she's looking for. I'm trying my best but she won't even look at me. What in God's name do I have to do to get her attention?'

Katherine rubbed her calf as I spoke and then picked up her towel to wipe the sweat off her neck.

'I'll tell you what we'll do. I'll come over here with you this evening and I'll see if I can help you get it right.'

We agreed to meet up after dinner and practise this seemingly elusive exercise together. Later that evening in the studio, Katherine placed her right hand on the barre and stretched her left leg out to the side.

'When you do a tendue, you bring your leg smoothly inwards. Well, the Russian style is to snap it back in very quickly and neatly as if it were an elastic band. That's what Svetlana wants you to do.'

Katherine proceeded to show me the Russian style and I could see an immediate difference. I stayed there practising until about ten o'clock when the cleaners locked up the school.

When I got back to my room Nicola was asleep, so I found my torch and Novena, and went out to the corridor to say my nightly prayers. When I finished I thought about my parents at home and how they had put so much effort and energy into getting me to Perm. I felt under enormous pressure to succeed, because I couldn't stand the thought of failing at ballet. I was so frightened that I wasn't good enough to be in the school and once again, the tears spilled down my cheeks. When I was worn out, I climbed into bed, cuddled up to my cabbage patch doll and fell promptly asleep.

Svetlana came into the class the next morning with her usual smile. She kicked off her shoe and indicated that we were to do a tendue. I flicked my leg out and snapped it back so fast that you could hardly see it. I felt exhilarated.

I knew it looked good and Svetlana turned to look at me as if she were in slow motion.

'Mon-i-ca! Mon-i-ca!'

She clapped her hands and stood watching me as I did the Russian style tendue. I couldn't keep the smile off my face as Svetlana watched in amazement. I think she was astonished that someone had finally understood what she was trying to say. She made the whole class look at me.

Every now and then she would dig her hands into my shoulders to adjust my position or to make me stand straighter, but she was delighted. You must remember that I was still a child. At the time, I couldn't believe it. I finally felt as if I turned the corner and I could be a success after all. As I got dressed after class, I started to feel optimistic about the future and actually looked forward to the rest of the year in Perm. When class ended I realised I was starving, so Donna and I ran down to the canteen on the ground floor. The canteen opened at midday for lunch, and although it was only ten minutes before noon, there were already about 20 kids outside the door screaming at the staff. Some of the older boys banged on the door, ran around the side to the kitchen window and shouted in at the cooks, 'Open the door. We're starving!'

It was frantic. I couldn't believe it. Until this point I had always lingered after ballet class and the canteen would be open by the time I got there. The queue was headed by three children who stood patiently and quietly amid the noise. Out of nowhere, a blonde-haired boy of around 17 years of age lifted them into the air one by one and placed them behind him in the queue. His friends who had been screaming in the window, then joined him at the top of the queue. The younger children looked extremely indignant, but they just turned around to each other and started nattering in Russian and glaring at the boys.

We stood at the back of the queue looking at this in wonder. I hadn't seen anything like it. On the stroke of twelve, we heard the door-bolt slide open and everyone cheered. The blonde boy then held everyone back, while his friends strutted in ahead of him. We finally made it as far as the counter to discover there was plenty of food for everyone, so I'm not sure why they made such a fuss. It was great fun though and I soon discovered this was a daily routine—one that never failed to make me laugh.

The canteen was a crazy place and always good for a laugh. Hygiene wasn't a priority. There were actually kittens born there and they were just left to run around.

Nobody bothered trying to get rid of them. If a burger was particularly nasty it was fed to the kittens.

But one of the strangest sights in the canteen was to see the children eating dinner with towels over their heads, or with their hoods up. Most people would have sweated so much during class that they would try to keep the heat in their heads. They were terrified they'd get swollen glands or a crick in their neck.

This habit of theirs came in handy later in the year, when I started to skip piano classes. I usually sat in the canteen with my hood up trying to hide from the piano teacher. Needless to say, it didn't work. She always caught me and brought me back to class.

Chapter Three

A group of women called *Mamoushkas* —*Mamoushka* means mother in Russian— looked after the students in the Internat. For some reason they all seemed to be big, burly types who commanded authority by their mere presence.

Throughout my years in the school, I never got to know any of them on a personal level, which was odd given their 'motherly' role.

They ensured we kept our rooms clean, went to bed and got up on time. They were also supposed to keep the boys on their own floor at night, though they weren't always successful in this regard. Every Sunday they inspected our bedrooms and graded us on them. I always made sure the room was spotless so I never got anything less than an A.

The *Mamoushkas* could be your friend or foe. They often spied on us and reported us to our teachers, which I would later learn to my detriment. The one thing I intensely disliked about them was that they assumed we were guilty until we were proven innocent. They favoured the boys and let them get away with murder.

Every morning a *Mamoushka* came onto the fifth floor to wake us up. We were supposed to be out of the Internat by nine o'clock but quite often we'd only be waking up at that time. The 'morning' *Mamoushka* had an extraordinarily high-pitched voice and would shout out in Russian as she walked up and down the corridor, '*Para Stavit!*' For the entire three years I was in school, I never understood what she said, but we all hated her. The poor woman was only shouting that it was time to get up, but she drove us crazy.

Before long we established a daily routine. Every morning I pulled on my pink tights and black leotard, donned my tracksuit and ran over to the canteen to see what was on offer for breakfast. It was generally just bread and tea, but I could only drink the tea. The bread was so hard you could stab someone with it.

Most mornings I ran back and tried to get some food from my room before they locked our floor for the day. Our floor was locked as soon as everyone went to class to prevent theft, as none of our rooms had individual locks. If I made it on time, I'd run up and grab a bar of chocolate from my suitcase, but often I would be too late and the *Mamoushka* wouldn't let me up. When this would happen I'd run around to the cake shop and buy some fresh pastries.

We discovered we had a wide array of subjects, much to the delight of the girls. I, however, was less enthused. I had changed from someone who didn't aspire to being a professional dancer to a person who was completely consumed and obsessed by ballet. My driving force was the desire to be as good as any Russian dancer. I wanted to wipe the frosty looks off their faces.

I went to Perm to study ballet and that was all I wanted to do. I didn't have a huge interest in other classes. They were just time fillers until I could get back to ballet. It's fair to say that I became very narrow-minded. I saved all my energy for dance classes. I was so competitive at ballet that I would make myself sick with worry. Subconsciously I knew I had the ability to be a professional ballet dancer if I gave it the time; it was all I wanted to do now.

Ballet took place every day from half past ten until noon. We had Russian language class three times a week from nine o'clock 'till ten o'clock. Nothing came easily in the early days, but Russian was the most difficult subject at the time. The language seemed so alien. The alphabet alone took a few months to become familiar with. It contains sounds as well as letters, and while the English alphabet can be learned in a song, the Russian alphabet is much more difficult.

We also had English twice a week at the start of the year but when it became apparent that our standard of English was higher than the teacher's, they dropped that class.

Gymnastics took place twice a week and I enjoyed it immensely even though it was often excruciating.

Sakharova's daughter was our teacher, although there weren't many similarities between them. Every now and then we'd see a flash of her mother in her when she would get annoyed. We were supposed to build endurance, flexibility, and strength in this class and the teacher seemed to delight in pushing us to the limits. One of her specialities was making her students do the 'suspended splits'. This meant that we would do the splits in a conventional manner, but our feet would be on two separate chairs. If you could lower your bum onto the floor, you automatically got a 5. In Russia, a 5 is equivalent to an A; a 4 is a B and so on. Donna and I were the lucky ones. We were the only Irish that could do this particular manoeuvre.

It seemed as if she tried to turn us inside out. Another exercise involved standing against a ladder that was nailed to the wall and lifting our left leg over 180 degrees as far to the right as possible. We would partner with another student, who would push our leg to breaking point. Donna and I always worked together and we tried to hit the three o'clock position every time. We were both obscenely flexible and extremely competitive. My party piece for the year was lying on my stomach and arching my back so I could rest my head on my bum.

French was a subject I found hard to take seriously. I had been to France on many occasions and had a decent grasp of the language and accent. Our French teacher was a Russian lady who had never left her native country or even conversed with a French person. She spoke French with a strong Russian accent, which I never got used to.

Historical dancing was a fun and relaxed class. Elena Kamenskaya taught us and she had a *laissez-faire* attitude to her Irish students. We did waltzes and polkas, and because there were no boys in the class, we just waltzed together and had a laugh.

On the other hand, I never got into character dancing. I wasn't a natural character dancer to say the least. I enjoyed watching it but I wasn't inspired by the music or movements.

Lidiya Ulanova was our character teacher and was probably the best teacher in the whole school. She was fabulous but I still didn't enjoy her class. Ulanova saw very quickly that I wasn't particularly interested and more or less ignored me for the year. At the beginning, I tried to immerse myself into the manner in which character should be danced, but she let me know that it wasn't to be my forte. I skipped a few classes in first year, but she never passed any comment. I think she understood I was so focused on ballet that I had left no room for anything else.

Music was the last class of the week. I had never studied it before, but they thought it would improve our musicality and rhythm. I've always been lucky enough to have a natural internal rhythm and I didn't need to read music to be a better ballet dancer. I had my first piano class at 14 and to be honest, I saw it as a waste of time. I had to spend many hours practising the piano to get to an acceptable level whereas I preferred to spend my time perfecting my ballet technique.

My piano class took place every Friday during lunch, but I spent most of my Friday lunches sitting between the girls with my hood pulled up, hoping the teacher wouldn't see me. I was the worst of the Irish girls at piano and it didn't really bother me. I was delighted to be able to sit down in front of the piano and play anything at all.

In the midst of all these classes, it was always at the back of our minds that we could be sent home at any time, and we'd have to get on with things and sit our Leaving Certificate. Therefore, I brought maths and science books with me and I'd often make myself sit down in the evening on my bed and read my science book.

A few weeks after arriving I brought my week's laundry down to the bathroom with my washing powder and set about hand-washing my clothes. There were no washing machines in the school and no hot water either. We had to wash our clothes in freezing cold water in big steel baths. I had never washed a sock before going to Perm, so I found it very tough. Nicola came with me and we discussed how things were going.

'It's much tougher than I thought, Nicola. What do you think?'

'It's not great. It's really strange how Svetlana just ignores us most of the time,' Nicola said, as she struggled to dissolve the washing powder, but she was wasting her time. The washing powder never dissolved because the water wasn't warm enough.

Nicola always wore gloves when she washed her clothes, so she put these on, picked up her pink tights and started scrubbing them with a look of determination.

'How on earth are we going to get these clean?' she asked in exasperation.

'I don't know!' I agreed, looking at my clothes in despair.

'They never smell clean anyway, no matter how much powder I put in. I wish I could give them to Mam and she'd be able to get them lovely and soft like she always does.'

I would get homesick when I least expected it. It would come at me from nowhere and hurt me in the pit of my stomach. There was a few minutes of silence while we watched the clothes steeping in water and pondered how easy life had been at home. I blinked several times so Nicola wouldn't see the tears welling in my eyes and set about washing my laundry with a new fury.

When we were done, we opened the doors to the drying room, which looked like a sauna with clothes lines and huge shelves. We left our clothes and returned to our bedroom where we sat down to darn our ballet shoes for the rest of the evening.

My leather ballet shoes had rapidly acquired holes in them from dancing on the rough wooden floor, so we spent about half an hour darning them every night. Although I didn't particularly like sewing, it was always a relaxing, ritualistic part of the evening.

That night we put the kettle on and drank hot chocolate while we darned and chatted. By nine o'clock Nicola was asleep like a clockwork doll. She never had any problems sleeping, no matter what happened.

After listening to her rhythmic breathing for about 15 minutes, and annoyed with myself for not being able to sleep, I crept out of the room and into the hall. I sat on the couch quietly thinking about home, and about how much I wanted to go back. At this point, I had my first panic attack. My breathing became very harsh and I started to cry. Ella heard me crying and came out of her room. She just put her arms around me and rocked me as she said,

'Shush . . . shush.'

'It's okay Monica. Calm down. What's wrong?'

'I . . . I . . . just miss . . . hic . . . home,' I sobbed, uncontrollably now that someone was showing me a little kindness.

'I know. Shush . . . it's okay. We all miss home.'

She took a bottle of Bach's Rescue Remedy out of her pocket and told me to put a few droplets on my tongue. It was a mixture of herbs that is supposed to calm you down and steady the nerves. Ella was only 17, but she was exactly the calming, motherly figure I needed at that time.

I hadn't spoken to her much as she had dashed around classes, but she had always taken time to smile at me and ask if I had settled in. I guess she saw a panic-stricken 14-year-old child walking around the halls of the school and decided to look out for me. 'You know, it's hard to get used to sleeping in a strange place, eating weird food, making new friends and trying to be the best at ballet, isn't it?'

'Yeah,' I agreed.

'And I have a funny feeling that someone here is very dedicated to ballet, is that right? I've seen you go over to the studio at night to practise.'

I kind of sobbed and laughed in agreement. I had been going over to the school every night on my own and spending two hours there trying to improve my technique.

I was very focused on improving week by week. I didn't set out to become the best in the class, but I set myself small, achievable goals every day.

Because Nicola and I had come from the same ballet school and were close in age, we were always compared to each other and Nicola was always deemed to be the better of the two. My first goal was to become better than Nicola, which was why I went on my own every other night. I usually stayed until half ten or eleven o'clock when the cleaners would ask me to leave.

'I just want to be good enough to stay on, Ella. I don't want to be sent home at the end of the year, even though I miss my family.'

'Don't worry, Monica. You'll be fine. Now, do you feel like getting some sleep? If you are feeling bad again, don't come out here and cry, just come in and have a chat with me, and I'll even give you some magic rescue remedy if you're lucky!'

I was fairly drained by this stage and I fell into a dreamless sleep immediately. For the next week or so I had a chat with Ella when I came back from practising ballet and gradually forgot about crying. When we would finish chatting, I'd get my torch and say my Novena in bed before going to sleep for the night.

About two weeks later Lidiya, one of the *Mamoushkas*, came on to our floor with what appeared to be a grey rag. She grabbed the first person she saw, which happened to be Ella.

'Do you know who owns these?' she asked, and with a flourish she plonked a pair of greyish-white knickers into Ella's hands.

Ella quickly glanced at the label and noting that they had been bought in Dunnes Stores said, 'Oh, they're one of ours. I don't know who owns them, but I'll take care of it.'

She looked at the size and figured they had to be mine. She came up to my room and said, 'Here you go,' and she twirled the knickers in the air. I blushed because I recognised the rainbow-coloured elastic immediately. I grabbed them out of her hands.

'What have you been up to?' Ella chuckled, as she watched me squirm.

'Nothing! Where did you get these?'

She told me the *Mamoushka* had them and it dawned on me that I must have dropped them on the way up the stairs. I was so embarrassed, but I hoped that no one had seen them. Ella told me she'd brought them straight to me.

Unfortunately, I wasn't to be that lucky, and James told me the next day how the *Mamoushka* had found my knickers hanging outside one of the boy's rooms. Someone had found them on the stairs and brought them to the second floor, where over 60 boys lived. They had done the rounds: they had been on the boys' heads, they were hung outside their doors—they had been everywhere.

Of course they soon discovered they were mine. No one else would fit into knickers made for young children. After that I stopped doing a weekly wash. I washed my clothes every other night and I never washed my underwear downstairs again.

The days turned into weeks and suddenly it was November. I couldn't believe how quickly the time had passed. I was thriving in ballet and continuing to do outlandish manoeuvres in gymnastics. Svetlana continued to blow hot and cold with all of us, and I was constantly in and out of her favour. Whenever I got sick of being ignored and I wanted Svetlana's attention, I just had to do the now infamous tendue on the barre and hope that she might notice.

By this stage, there was such an intense and competitive environment in the school that everyone kept on falling out. I was hard to live with. I was deeply competitive and didn't care about anything but ballet. I was restless at night and if I can remember correctly, I was short with people.

I in turn found it hard to live with Nicola after a while. She wore a mask when she cleaned the room and gloves when she washed her clothes. She also wore an eye mask when she fell asleep. We were both very homesick and the atmosphere and mood in the room was depressing.

It was such a competitive environment that whoever I lived with would have eventually gotten on my nerves, and I on theirs. We bickered and quarrelled constantly and it didn't help that we had no space for time alone. Somebody was always fighting with someone, and there was constant bitching. We fought amongst ourselves all the time. There was nothing too serious in it. It was just a bunch of teenage girls thrown into a melting pot of competition.

Life soon developed a familiar routine of classes, ballet, and washing. I continued to feel very homesick, though, and I looked forward to the weekly phone call from my parents. They rang at the same time every Sunday, and we'd spend about 30 minutes chatting. There was only one phone in the Internat, located on the ground floor. We could only receive calls on it; we weren't able to dial out.

If we were expecting a phone call, we had to sit by the phone and wait for it to ring, because if someone else answered, they wouldn't fetch us.

Mam generally spoke to me for about 25 minutes and then she'd let Dad talk to me for about five minutes at the end. Siobhán and Eileen usually grabbed the phone for a few minutes in the middle of Mam's chat if they were around. We always had great conversations as we used the time to talk properly.

If I was feeling homesick I deliberately kept my voice bright and never let them know how lonely I was feeling. I was torn between desperately wanting to go home and desperately wanting to succeed as a ballet dancer. Mam asked me the very same questions every week.

'Are you sleeping well? Now tell me the truth!

'How's the food? Make sure to eat to keep up your strength.

'How are you doing in class?

'Are you okay for money?'

I reassured her that things couldn't be better and we said our goodbyes. I promised I would try to write a letter soon. I think she hung up after those conversations feeling more at ease but I usually got a pang of homesickness after talking to them, and it took a while to bounce back.

Chapter Four

In the first week of December when Nicola and I were in our room getting ready for bed, Nicola was making some hot chocolate. She poured the boiling water into her cup and went to put the kettle back on its cradle but didn't look at what she was doing. The kettle fell off the window sill and the freshly boiled water spilled all over her thighs.

She was only wearing knickers and a vest, so she had no protection. Nicola started screaming and sat looking in horror at her legs. I jumped into action immediately. I grabbed her dressing gown off the bed and threw it around her. 'Come on! Come on! You're grand.' I tried to get her to the bathroom to put cold water on her legs as soon as possible. But as Nicola hobbled towards the door, some of the Irish girls, who had heard the commotion, came through it. Nicola toppled back and I caught her from behind.

'STOP! Stop pushing the door,' I screamed, as I tried to protect Nicola. More heads appeared and there was utter confusion and chaos as everyone tried to find out what was wrong. There was no room to bring Nicola out and we were losing precious time.

'FUCK OFF!' I screamed at everyone, as I pulled Nicola through the door behind me towards the bathroom. I doused her legs with cold water and the girls who had followed us joined in. Her skin started coming off in large pieces and I began to fret. She had only received the burns a minute ago but everything seemed to have moved in slow motion and it felt like much longer. Some of the girls were giving out to me for cursing at them. But all I wanted to do was help Nicola. I didn't waste time with explanations.

One of the *Mamoushkas* came up to the bathroom when she heard the commotion and she took control of the situation from there.

Nicola had received second degree burns and was sent to hospital in Perm, where she spent the night. When she was released, she was so sore that she couldn't make it up and down the stairs, so she remained in the sick bay on the ground floor for a week.

When her mother heard she wasn't improving she arranged to have her sent home. Nicola was delighted. She had been miserable because she could do nothing. She had difficulty moving one of her legs and was beginning to worry. When I found out she was going home, Claire Rooney and I packed her bags and brought them down to sick bay.

We packed the most comfortable clothes we could find, so they wouldn't irritate her burns. She was the first girl to leave. I still remember her departure. She left the Internat at half past four in the morning about ten days before Christmas. We were all so relieved for her because she needed her parents' care. We didn't have any emotional support in the school. It was all about ballet and discipline and when you're a sick child, there's nothing you want more than to have your mother and father hug you and tell you that everything will be okay.

Nicola looked genuinely happy and excited for the first time in ages. All the Irish students got up when it was time for her to leave. We hugged her and wished her well on her journey back, though to be honest, we were slightly jealous that we weren't going home as well. She'd be back in time for Christmas, while we wouldn't be returning until after the New Year. James and Elena brought Nicola to the train station in Perm and as they drove off, we all started singing 'Olé! Olé! Olé!' and woke the entire building before we were ushered back to our rooms by one of the *Mamoushkas*.

I had gotten to know a Ukrainian girl called Natasha during the first few months. We often read our books on the couch in the hall and had become very friendly. Natasha was under the instruction of Elena Bystritskaya in ballet while her two room-mates trained under Lidiya Ulanova.

Ulanova taught ballet as well as character but she only took the better students for ballet. There was some tension in Natasha's room as she felt the other girls looked down on her.

I liked Natasha at once. She taught me Russian words and songs whenever we met. When I had an empty room, I offered her Nicola's bed so she could have a break from her room-mates' remarks. She jumped at the chance and moved in the following day.

It was great because she was like a breath of fresh air. It was refreshing to spend time with her and get insights into her life, and the workings and politics of the school. She was in her seventh year of schooling and knew the system and the teachers inside out.

Natasha was slightly older than me. She was 17-years old and was picked on by the other girls because she was slightly overweight. She was an extremely pretty girl with blonde curly hair that fell to her shoulders. She came from a very poor family. Her mother was a cleaner while her father was a member of the KGB.

We spent hours learning to communicate and chatting about our respective backgrounds. This period helped my language skills a lot as Natasha had very little English, so we conversed mainly in Russian. I enjoyed living with my new friend and I still spent a lot of time with the Irish girls, so everything worked out really well.

Although we were spending our first Christmas away from home, we tried to keep things as normal as possible. Four days before Christmas the Irish students decided to go shopping for presents. We put on our plastic boots, our eiderdown jackets and headed out into a snowstorm. The Russians always wore fur from head to toe during the winter. You could only buy natural materials in Russia back then, so we stood out a mile with our synthetic ensembles.

There was a souvenir shop very near the theatre, which was just down the road from the Internat, so we went straight there to bring a flavour of Russia home to our parents. I pulled my blue hood close to my face as we ventured out into the freezing air. Donna and I linked arms and walked quickly across the road to the shops. The children from the ballet school always linked arms when they walked around Perm so they were immediately identifiable as ballet students. However, we were warned not to go out alone, because people in the city weren't used to seeing foreigners.

Stalin had closed a number of Russian cities to outsiders during the 1930s, including Perm. These cities even disappeared off the maps as they were often used for making weapons.

Perm itself is an industrial city and is famous for its Mig fighting planes. The city had just opened to foreigners in 1990 and ballet students were some of the first allowed in. The snow was so thick that I could barely see my feet in front of me but we kept a steady pace and we were soon in the cosy gift shop. It was filled with *Matrioshka* dolls of all sizes and colours and had an amazing array of junk, which we gleefully looked through, before buying the most predictable items. I bought *Matrioshka* dolls for Eileen and Mam, and splashed out on some ethnic vodka for Dad while Siobhán got a brooch. The others bought similar items.

They didn't have bags in the shop so the assistant just wrapped everything in brown paper and deposited them into my arms. When we finished shopping I pulled my hood over my head to protect me from the heavy snowfall.

My arms were so full that I couldn't link them, so I hunched over and walked a pace or two ahead of the other girls.

As I crossed the road I heard Emma scream at me to stop. 'MONICA, LOOK OUT!' From the corner of my eye I saw a set of headlights coming towards me. I thought that I would make it across the road on time, so I rushed ahead. I was wrong though, and before I knew it, I felt a dull thud on the side of my leg.

Everything seemed to happen in slow motion from that point. I was thrown into the air and I could see my legs splayed out in front of me. My back hit the windscreen just before I fell to the ground. The only thing I could think about was not to let the car hit the back of my head.

I thought I would die if I didn't get up immediately. The car wouldn't be able to stop because of the snow and ice. I landed on my backside in front of the car. I jumped up as soon as I hit the ground, not fully understanding what had happened. I saw the smashed windscreen, bent bonnet and broken headlight and thought, 'Oh shit! I'm in trouble now.'

I glanced across at the other girls. They were standing on the side of the road with stricken expressions on their faces.

The driver was sitting in the car looking at me in shock. I thought he would report me to the assistant director of the school, Ninel Pidemskaya, and I would get in trouble for being careless. I screamed across to the girls, 'Pick up my dolls. Pick up my dolls,' and I started to run towards the Internat. Donna and Claire grabbed my parcels and started running behind me.

The driver must have thought he had run into a bunch of mad children as he watched eight girls wearing plastic boots and various coloured jackets run after me.

'You're grand, you're grand,' I repeated continuously to myself as I ran up the stairs. It was like a mantra that kept me calm. I was so intent on getting back before the driver could find me that I took the stairs three at a time. My ears were ringing and the adrenaline raced through my blood. When I reached the safety of my room I tore off my coat and boots, and sat on the bed waiting for the others to arrive.

I didn't really know how I felt. In truth, I didn't feel any pain at that point and I was relieved that I didn't break any bones, though I was still terrified I would get into trouble for damaging the car. I sat on my own for about five minutes wondering what was taking the girls so long. All at once they piled into the room and some of them started crying when they saw me.

'Are you okay, Monica?' Donna asked, looking at me in tears. She was physically shaking and was as white as a ghost.

'You were thrown about six feet into the air. You could have been killed.'

'I feel fine . . . I think!'

The girls were more shocked than I was. Some of them got down on their knees and said a prayer of thanks. I couldn't understand why they were so shaken.

'I'm fine; I'm grand, don't worry.'

'You're in shock, that's what's wrong with you,' Katherine proclaimed and she put a kettle on to boil so I could have some sweet tea.

'It's a bloody miracle! It must be that Novena of yours that saved you, because nothing else could have,' Emma added.

Everyone looked so shocked and upset that I felt I should be crying, so I sniffed a little and tried to cry. As I began to relax I realised that my hip was sore, so I stood up and stretched to see if I genuinely was okay.

Gradually the girls trickled back to their rooms. When I woke up the next morning, my hip was extremely painful and the coccyx bone in my bum felt as if I had splintered it.

Our exams were coming up at the end of the month and I was beginning to angst that I wouldn't be able to do the ballet exam. I couldn't get out of bed without aching all over so I stayed in my room. Donna came in to see how I was feeling.

'Donna, I can't move. I think I broke the bone in my bum. I can't get out of bed,' I said, with a tremor in my voice. 'How the hell am I going to do my exam? Sacky is coming in to see us.'

We had begun to refer to Sakharova as 'Sacky' amongst ourselves. It wasn't until much later we learnt that sacky means 'urine' in Russian.

'Don't worry, you'll be fine. Take two aspirin and stay in bed and I'll tell Svetlana that you're sick. I think a hotwater bottle might help.'

She filled a hot-water bottle and told me to keep it on my bum at all times. I took her advice to heart and strapped it to me like a saddle. Every time I left the room to use the toilet, I could hear the girls giggling after me. Svetlana came to visit me after class that day. Through a mixture of sign language and bad Russian I told her that I fell off the window sill and landed on the locker. I tried to explain that I'd be back to class in a day or two. I was so afraid of the teachers that I down-played my injury. We got into trouble for the simplest of things and there was no way I was going to tell her that I got knocked down.

As she listened to my unlikely story I wasn't sure if she believed me or not. She appeared sympathetic and I felt bad for lying to her but I couldn't take the chance that Pidemskaya might find out.

Carols echoed through the corridor of the fifth floor during the month of December. The Irish group came together to create a festive atmosphere to keep our spirits high.

Classes continued as normal and I was glad to keep busy as it kept me from missing home too much.

Normally at this time of year I would be out shopping with Mam and enjoying the smells and treats that I always associated with Christmas. I loved going into O'Connell Street, seeing the fairy lights and hinting at the presents I wanted.

On our first Christmas Eve in Perm we held a huge party for our Russian friends. They were mainly of the Russian Orthodox faith and celebrated Christmas on 7 January. Their big winter celebration was the New Year. While Communism dominated Russia, people weren't allowed to celebrate religious feast days, so our young friends, who had lived most of their lives under this regime, barely understood our concept of Christmas.

That night we shared what remained of our treats and had a feast like no other. Everyone emptied their stash and we put chocolate, cheese, butter, mayonnaise, fresh bread and fizzy drinks on the table for all to share.

The music boomed from the stereo all evening. We drew a picture of a crib and hung it on the corridor wall. At midnight we gathered around and sang carols.

It was a poignant occasion for all the Irish as we missed our families desperately. The Russians were mesmerised by how vulnerable and emotional we were. They had toughened up by living away from home for so long. Most of them had been in the school for years. That night I grew very teary-eyed as we stood and sang *Oíche Ciúin*. We finished up the evening and went to bed dreaming of home.

I woke up the next morning to hear James running into our rooms wishing everyone a 'Happy Christmas'. He brought a rave tape that had arrived in the post and played it on Donna's stereo. He pushed the volume up high and let it blare down the hall. Waking up to the Prodigy was an unusual start to Christmas morning for most of us.

Because we were in Russia, we missed most of the dance music craze that was sweeping through Ireland. I was a fan of pop music when I left, but then again, I had just turned 14.

We went to ballet class and afterwards decided to go to Mass in the nearest church. When we arrived into the church building we almost stumbled across three open coffins that were in the middle of the room. There are no seats or aisles in Russian churches, so the coffins were the focal point that morning. The church was thronged with mourners and we found ourselves jostled up to the bodies, where we did our best to look sombre and sad.

Everyone was very giddy. We couldn't believe we were attending a Russian funeral on Christmas Day. It was so bizarre. It felt odd. We lit a few candles and hurried out of the church as soon as we could.

Elena, our Russian teacher, had invited us to her apartment for Christmas dinner. We arrived, starving as usual, and it was such a treat to smell the home-cooked fare. We gave her presents and sat around the table, which was laden with delicious food. We were trying desperately not to grab it and start eating immediately because it all looked so great. Her husband came into the room dressed as Santa and gave us all a small present. I was very touched as I knew they must have spent a lot of time and money on us.

Russian people always put on a great spread for their guests, even when they can't afford it. They are very generous people and this hospitality is extended to everyone, not only to foreigners. We ate so much food that I thought they would have nothing left for themselves. In this regard, it was embarrassing, but I had survived my first Christmas in Russia and it wasn't that bad.

The time passed quickly until New Year's Eve when our mid-year ballet exam was taking place. My coccyx was still giving trouble and I had difficulty dancing. My right hip clicked every time I lifted my leg above 90 degrees. I was very conscious of the fact that Sakharova was attending the class to see how we were progressing so I didn't want to mess up.

I took two aspirin before the class began so I wouldn't be hindered by any pain. I got through the exam but I was very self-conscious about the sound of my hip, but no one seemed to notice.

Halfway through the class Sakharova stood up and announced she was leaving. She seemed to have had enough.

'Congratulations. You should be very proud of yourselves,' she said, in a half-hearted manner.

We were thrilled though and this lacklustre comment enthused us enough to look forward to returning the following term.

Chapter Five

Coming back to Ireland was an emotional experience. I arrived home to Dublin airport to find all my aunties and uncles, Mam, Dad, and my sisters Siobhán and Eileen waiting for me. There was a real party atmosphere and everyone was so excited to see me. I couldn't believe they were making such a fuss but I was genuinely delighted to see them. My family had held Christmas dinner off for me, and the day after I came home, we had the full Christmas dinner, with turkey, pudding and crackers. It was wonderful. I couldn't believe how much glorious food there was. I spent the entire two weeks in front of the television, eating as much as I could.

My mother couldn't believe the change in me. I had been such a finicky eater before I left; now I would eat anything she put in front of me, and more. The only exercise I got during that holiday was using the remote control. I did nothing. Mam washed and ironed my clothes, which was such a luxury. All my clothes smelt of stagnant water. I was never able to get them perfectly clean in Perm but when Mam gave them back to me, they were lovely and soft, and smelt of fabric conditioner.

Just before I returned to Perm, I started to get nervous again. I lay awake in bed for the last two nights at home. I couldn't sleep at all and my panic attacks returned. I was so nervous about going back. All too soon, however, I was on my way to the airport. Mam and Dad brought me to the Aeroflot check-in counter and I greeted the other girls, who didn't look half as nervous as I felt. As I stood in line, my lungs started to constrict and I felt as if I couldn't breathe.

I managed to conceal this, but when the time came for me to go through the departure gates, and I saw the others saying their goodbyes, I went to pieces and started to cry. Mam and Dad looked at each other in concern.

'Are you okay, pet? You know you don't have to go if you don't want to,' Mam gently said, as she stroked my face.

'It's true,' Dad added. 'You can always come home with us. We won't mind if you decide not to go back. There's no shame in that.'

I kept on crying and didn't say anything. John Baraldi was about to go through the departure gates when he turned around and saw me with tears streaming down my face. He came back and put his arm around my shoulder.

'Come on, Monica. You'll be okay.'

He nodded at my parents as if to say that he'd look after me and brought me towards the gates. I gulped back the tears, waved at my parents, and walked off without looking back.

The rest of the journey to Perm went fairly smoothly, and as soon as I was back in the Internat I felt fine. Nicola returned to the school and I was glad to have her back, but I was surprised to discover that Catherine Loane chose not to return. Everyone seemed happy to see us and the Russian girls were friendlier. They seemed to take us more seriously when they saw we had come back for more.

We were moved into a bigger classroom on our return after Christmas, which I interpreted as a good sign—I thought the teachers were now taking us more seriously.

The Russians had started classes two days before our arrival, so we had to get into the swing of things very quickly. A few days later I was darning my shoes and wondering why I had been crying in the airport. Everything started to make sense. Although things were pretty competitive in ballet class, I was content in my environment and getting on with my peers. Looking back on it now it seems that I fluctuated between being ecstatically happy to be there and being utterly miserable, but at the time I was just a 14-year-old girl with ordinary mood swings in extraordinary circumstances.

I think I was hungry for the entire first year in school. One of my main concerns was getting food that I could eat. I brought over as much food as I could carry from Ireland because I still couldn't eat most of the food served in the canteen.

My abiding memory of that place is the cabbage and burgers. The cabbage was first boiled and then fried with carrots and onions, and it tasted delicious. I loved it, but I never got used to the burgers. They looked like big meatballs and every time I cut into one, a stench came out; it was just awful. The odd day we had *kasha* (porridge) or buckwheat instead of cabbage and luckily I enjoyed them too.

Occasionally they'd have milk soup on the menu. It was a mixture of water and milk with chicken stock and spaghetti. Other times they'd have *borch*, which is a traditional Russian dish. It's like beetroot soup with meat and vegetables and it was delicious.

On rare occasions they served chicken. Students would receive about 100 grammes of chicken on a plate. It would be diced into about 20 pieces. I'm sure the leg was even cut in half. Everyone would want the breast so there would be fights for it, otherwise you'd be left with the stringy bits with the bone. I've seen arguments in the canteen over food—the guys would often steal some bread, or take food from the younger children. The Russians have unique culinary habits. Some Russian students used to put jam into their tea and I thought this was one of the strangest things I had ever seen. Like everything else, though, I soon got used to it and then I grew to love it. I started putting jam in my tea before long.

It happened very seamlessly, but I was gradually becoming more like the Russians. I suppose I was at such an impressionable age, that I slipped easily into their culture and traditions. Sometimes now I catch myself thinking in Russian, and I realise how much the country is a part of me.

Most of the Irish girls seemed fine with the canteen food, but I was just particularly picky, so I started going to the *gastronome*, which is a Russian version of a supermarket. I must admit that I never got used to the queues of people waiting to buy food. When I would go to the *gastronome*, I might have to queue for an hour just to get in the door. Most of the food would be gone by the time I got there, however, but the Russians couldn't afford the foreign food, so that was always left. I bought anything remotely edible that I could find.

I went there every single day. The chocolate bars were stored behind a glass case. You couldn't actually pick them up—you could only look at them. The Russians love to look at things, so I would have to force my way through the crowd to where the chocolate was kept and I'd count how many bars they had out on display. If there were seven bars, I'd go up to the lady at the cash register and point at the cabinet and say 'Seven.' The shop assistant would inevitably look at me as if she didn't understand, and she generally got annoyed with me, so I'd write it down and hand her the piece of paper. She'd look at it and say, 'What do you want?'

'Chocolate,' I'd reply, as I would point towards the cabinet. The people in the queue behind me would be looking at me with a mixture of disgust and envy. I hated it.

There wasn't a big range of food. The shop sold cherry apples that were so small they were just skin and pips. There was no flesh on them at all, but these were treats, as you could only get them in the summer. You couldn't get fruit in the winter at all.

In Russia, everything is measured and sold by weight, so if you want to buy cheese or butter, you ask for 300 grammes of it, rather than picking up a lump of butter. Every weekend Donna and I started having 'bread and cheese' parties. We'd calculate how much 300 grammes of butter should cost and we'd bring our money down to the supermarket. Our Russian teacher, Elena, minded our money for us. Every Thursday, I went to her after class and told her that I needed to change $10, so she would go to the bank and give me the equivalent in rubles. We would get around 2000 rubles for $10, which was enough money to buy food for a week. She was so worried about us getting robbed that she did all this in her own time; she always gave us receipts for every transaction and treated us as if we were her own children.

Once we had our money in our pockets, we would buy the biggest lump of cheese that we could find. We always bought a Russian hard cheese which had a lovely, mild flavour, similar to Cheddar. I will always recall watching in anticipation as they weighed out the cheese and wrapped it in wax paper.

We would then get some deliciously fresh bread, and Donna and I would eat an entire loaf smothered with mayonnaise and sandwiched around the cheese. When I was starving during the week, I would fantasise about our next bread and cheese party and the sheer thought of it would keep me going until I had it for real.

We all had our own idiosyncrasies. Donna and I ate lots of Polish baby food, as well as bread and cheese. Claire Rooney used to mix Nesquik with water and eat it off the spoon like chocolate. Some of the girls bought Russian powdered milk which we would mix with sugar and water to make a paste.

I would eat anything. One time I had a packet of Shredded Wheat in my suitcase that had gone off and I was so hungry that I got some Easy Cheese slices that were also past their sell-by date, and ate them like a sandwich.

The Russian girls were lucky because they used to buy tinned food, but we wouldn't have known if we were buying cat food, so we generally steered clear of that. If I found something I liked, I'd try to memorise what the tin looked like. We tried to buy tins of condensed milk but you couldn't get them in the *gastronome*. Traders used to sell them at the side of the road like a contraband item, however, and I would eat a tin of that a day if possible.

I would also buy eight or nine éclairs at a time. The girls in the shop always put them in clear plastic bags and when I would get back to the Internat the girls would look at the bag and say, 'That's not normal.'

I knew some of them were on diets and they thought I was doing it to show off. The truth is that I was finding it hard to do the day-to-day things because I had lost so much weight. I was becoming very stressed over it. I just couldn't put on weight.

The *Mamoushkas* and the staff at the school were very conscious of keeping the girls and the boys separated from each other in the sleeping areas. There was a strict rule that boys weren't allowed onto the fifth floor and we weren't allowed into their rooms on the second floor. At night, the *Mamoushka* that looked after the boys locked them onto the floor before she retired for the night. She believed the boys went to bed each night and slept soundly.

This couldn't have been further from the truth. The boys had copies of the keys and were able to come and go as they pleased. One night, when I had just come back from practising in school, I heard the sound of flip-flops in the corridor outside my room. Then I heard the sound of muffled talking and laughing behind the door, which gradually got louder and louder. Nicola awoke with a start.

'What's going on, Monica?' she whispered.

'I don't know. I think some of the boys are on the floor.'

I picked up my torch and we crept silently towards the door in the dark. I was afraid to put on the light in case some of them came into our room. By this stage they had given up all pretences of keeping quiet, and they were shouting at each other and laughing out loud. I opened the door quietly and shone my torch down the corridor.

The floor was black with bodies. There were so many boys on the floor that they had no room to move and they were squashed up against the walls.

They were wearing cycling shorts, tracksuit bottoms, flip-flops and some of them looked as if they had been literally dragged out of bed to come up to our floor. Some of them had bottles of beer in their hands while the rest of them were just laughing and pushing each other. From the other end of the corridor I heard the *Mamoushka* screaming as she flipped the lightswitch on.

Suddenly the boys started running into the girls' rooms to hide, so Nicola and I stood with our backs to the door to make sure they couldn't enter our room. Some of them just stood brazenly on the floor and waited until they were sent back. These were the talented ones; they never got in trouble no matter what. The *Mamoushkas* ushered them back to their own floor, while the rest of the boys hid under beds or in wardrobes. They had to stay there for the rest of the night as they couldn't risk getting caught.

Chapter Six

When I look back on my first year in Russia, the most dramatic thing that happened was not my ballet tuition, but how I became so independent at such a young age. This became apparent when my family visited Perm in April that year. I was a different person to the young girl who had left Dublin.

I was independent and I relied on no one. I found it difficult to take instructions from my mother and father. In some ways, their visit put a strain on me, because suddenly the roles had changed and I had to look after them and show them around.

I was too self-obsessed and consumed by ballet. I didn't want any distractions, although at the same time, I was delighted to see them. I was changing from a child to an adult, and my parents found it difficult to accept. They only stayed five days, so they were gone before things became too tense.

Soon after our parents went home, Nicola got a rash that wouldn't go away so she was sent straight to the hospital in Perm. The doctors thought it was scarlet fever and didn't want to take any chances. Once again she was sent home to recover. And once again, Claire and I packed her bags.

It was shortly after Nicola left that boys began to take an interest in me. It happened overnight. I noticed one of the Mongolian boys catching my eye in the corridors and in the canteen. There were lots of students from Mongolia in the school. This boy was tall and broad, and had black hair with nice friendly eyes, so when he asked me one day if I wanted to go to the cinema, I said I would. His name was Gonserique.

The cinema consisted of an old television on stilts. We sat on hard chairs and I spent more time looking around in shock than at the film. Russian television isn't subtitled so I really didn't know what was going on in the film, but I was fairly excited anyway because I was on my first date.

He was 18 and far too old for me, but he seemed very protective. He dropped me to my room after the cinema and went back to his own room on the second floor. The next morning, he came up to me in the canteen and handed me a bag. When I looked inside there was a brand new pair of pointe shoes.

'Gonserique, I can't take these,' I said to him in a mixture of Russian and English, and I handed them back to him, but he pushed them towards me again.

'Take them,' he smiled. 'I like you.'

'I like you too,' I said, not knowing where to look.

He escorted me to ballet class that morning and when I finished, he was waiting for me. This soon became a pattern and he started to accompany me everywhere. I didn't know what to do as I had never had a boyfriend before, and I hated the way he was always there when I turned around. I didn't know how to handle him. He gave me little presents every few days and I never got anything for him. I wasn't able to say I didn't like being escorted everywhere, as if I was his property.

One day I was talking to James in the canteen when Gonserique came in and sat beside me. He threw his arm around my shoulder and glared at James, who in turn looked surprised.

'See you later, Monica,' he said, looking at me in puzzlement.

Gonserique grabbed my two shoulders and said, 'You're with me.'

Unlike my sisters and friends at home, I had to learn the trials of life without parental guidance. I learnt about relationships through trial and error and didn't have anyone to ask advice from.

I wasn't sure what to do about Gonserique, as I didn't like him that much. I wasn't interested in having a boyfriend. I just thought he was a nice boy, but I couldn't handle this possessive behaviour.

I had only gone to the pictures with him about two weeks previously, but he seemed to think we were dating. That evening I told him I didn't want to go out with him anymore. When he realised I was finishing with him, he was absolutely distraught and looked genuinely upset, so I tried to make it easier on him. I said I wanted to concentrate on my ballet and maybe we could get back together after the summer. I was sure that he'd forget all about me over the summer and he'd probably fall in love with someone else.

It was true that I wanted to concentrate on my ballet. I was beginning to feel the pressure, as we would find out at the end of the year who would get invited back to the school.

We weren't invited to return automatically, so I worked hard. I wanted to come back so badly. I became even more focused than ever and concentrated on preparing for my exams.

I spent every spare hour I had practising the piano, as it was the first exam on our list. I didn't want to fail anything, as I was afraid it would mean I wouldn't be invited back.

I played my exam piece, called 'Morning' non-stop for about six weeks until I knew it inside out. On the day of the piano exam, I got through it without problems and to my relief I passed.

On the day of the ballet exam, I was standing at the back barre thinking, 'I have to be better than everyone else.' I was nervous, but focused and excited as well. About seven or eight of the teachers streamed in and sat on the bench in front of the mirror. Sakharova, Ulanova, our teacher, Svetlana, and some of the other character and ballet teachers also watched us.

At the start of class we curtsied to the teachers and took our places at the barre. We did a series of pliés, tendues, fondues, ronde de jambes, relevés, adagios, and grande battements.

We then left the barre and performed the *Dance of the Hours*. Sakharova left at this point; she had seen enough. She didn't have to see the whole class to see what we could do.

When we finished, we gave a little bow and the teachers clapped and left the room. We would receive the results of the exam in the next hour, so we all stood around the classroom anxiously, waiting and wondering how we did. I wasn't sure how well I had performed. I didn't think I was any better than the other Irish girls, but I did feel I stood out in certain combinations. My mouth was dry and I could feel my heart rattling as I waited for Svetlana to come back with our marks.

'*Devochky, devochky.* You all did very well. Very good. You are all invited back to the school next year.'

She then proceeded to give out the marks. There was a silence for a minute and then everyone quickly left the room. The most important thing to me was that I was invited back; this was crucial, rather than the mark

I received. The fact that I received a 5 was a bonus. The rest of the exams paled into insignificance once I knew I was coming back to the school next year.

Once the exams were over, we started practising for a show we were due to perform a few weeks later in the National Concert Hall, Dublin. John Baraldi was bringing us back for a home-coming performance.

I was dancing in the corps de ballet of *Swan Lake* and I had a small solo part in a piece called *La Gioconda*. This is a very old dance that is hardly ever performed in the west.

It consists of three groups with four girls in each. I was in a group with three Russian girls and we were the only group to dance *La Gioconda* from the start to the finish. Some of the other girls were dancing parts from *The Nutcracker*. Ella and James were dancing the *Flower Festival in Genzano*, and Katherine was dancing the Russian from *The Nutcracker*, which is a character part.

We performed in the school theatre in Perm before we left for Dublin and the teachers were very happy with us.

I wasn't nervous about going on stage as we had practised so much that I was very sure of my moves. We locked our books, our woolies and personal items in our bedside lockers, so our bags were much lighter on the journey back.

There was great excitement going home. We were asked if we would take some of the Russian girls to stay in our houses for the National Concert Hall shows, so two girls, Anya and Xenia, stayed with me. They were both fabulous dancers. Xenia's mother worked in the theatre in Perm and Xenia later went on to become a soloist in the Kirov.

Mam and Dad collected us from the airport, but this time they were on their own. It was very exciting being home and I hugged them tightly for ages. We brought the Russian girls back to the house and they couldn't believe how different my life in Ireland was. Hot showers were a novelty for them.

Anya and Xenia stayed a week. During the week, my mother said that it was impossible to keep fruit in the house. The Russian girls loved it and ate us out of house and home, because it was almost impossible to buy fruit in Russia back in 1993. If you managed to buy a banana, it would be black, as if it had been baked.

We had three performances in the National Concert Hall and then we performed in University Concert Hall, Limerick. It was very well received and everyone was delighted, because it looked so professional. You wouldn't have thought that everyone in it was under 18 years of age.

At the end of the week the Russians returned to Perm and things got back to normal at home.

All the Irish students who had been in Perm booked into an advanced ballet class at Digges Lane Studios in Dublin city. A man called Gavin Dorrian taught the classes and he was fantastic. His classes were probably the best I have ever attended.

There were about 30 people in the class and there was hardly room to move, but it was a lovely place to dance. Although the studios had lovely floors and huge rooms, it seemed old and dusty. When we were dancing in Digges Lane, there was great excitement in the building because Boyzone were rehearsing in one of the studios and Michael Flatley was practising in another studio.

Someone told me they were practising Irish dancing to perform in next year's Eurovision contest, though I have to admit, I said that it would never take off. Once I saw it, however, I was impressed. Even the Russians looked at us with a new respect. A whole craze for Irish dancing started in Perm as a direct result of *Riverdance*; the Russians couldn't understand how we didn't know our own national dance.

At the end of the summer I found out who wasn't returning to Perm. Claire Rooney, Caitriona Lowry,

Ella Clarke and my old room-mate, Nicola McCarthy didn't return. Katherine O'Malley had graduated from the school and she took a job in a ballet company, Tartarstan in Kazan.

That left just a handful: Donna Addie, Emma O'Kane, Anna Moore, Claire Keating, James Dunne and me.

Some new students joined us on our second trip. Gillian Balmer and Darina Crean were invited, along with Emily and Antonia Boyle, who were twins.

A new boy also joined us, called Gavin du Paor, so now there were two boys as part of the Irish contingency.

Chapter Seven

When we returned to Perm to begin our second year of schooling, one of the *Mamoushkas* met us on the ground floor and told us that our rooms had been tampered with.

She said that from now on, we would be living on the third floor with the Russian children. I wasn't sure what she meant by 'tampered' so I ran up to my old room to see what had happened.

The door on the bedside locker was swinging open and my books and tapes were gone. I could see that my photographs were still there but anything of value had been taken. I couldn't understand why on earth anyone would have wanted to steal an English science book. Donna and I decided to share a room and I quickly ran down to the third floor to pick out a suitable double room.

I have to admit that I was glad to be back. I dumped my luggage on my bed and made my way into the corridor to see where everyone else was.

There was a large piece of plywood in the middle of the corridor separating our rooms from the children's rooms. It looked odd because we could only access the floor via the staircase on the left. All the Irish girls were in this cordoned off area, while James and Gavin were on the second floor with the boys. There was only one Russian on our floor, Natasha Balakhnicheva, and she shared a room with Claire. This year we were able to lock our individual rooms, so the floor was left open at all times, which gave us much more freedom.

John Baraldi had accompanied us on the trip once again and he called us into Emma's room.

'I have the list of the classes you're in, so listen carefully. Monica and Emma—you're in Lidiya Ulanova's class. Donna and Anna—Elena Bystritskaya. Claire—Ludmilla Sakharova. James—Alexandr Sakharov. Emily and Antonia—Nina Petrova Costrova. Gavin—Yuri Sidorov. Any questions?'

Nobody said anything. We were already thinking about how the classes would be. I couldn't help beaming.

Ulanova was one of the best teachers in the school while Bystritskaya could be very abrasive. She had a screechy voice that was hard to listen to for more than two minutes and she looked more like an old granny than a classical ballet teacher. She always wore woolly jumpers with a long skirt and baggy nylon tights. I looked forward to joining Ulanova's class.

Everyone dispersed soon afterwards and Donna and I went into our room. About an hour later while I was unpacking, James ran into to our room laughing loudly.

'Oh, Monica! You are never going to believe this. Gonserique is over in the school and he has your name written all over his jeans and t-shirt!'

'What? What do you mean?' I screeched, jumping off the bed.

'He's written your name in black marker all over his clothes.'

'Ohmigod! Where is he?' I screamed as I ran out.

'He's walking around the school,' James shouted after me, still laughing.

I was terrified the teachers would see this and think there was something going on. I was very mindful of the age gap. I didn't want to get a bad reputation in the school, especially considering the relationship between us was so innocent. I found him in the first floor corridor and dragged him up to our changing room.

Before I could say anything, he thrust a bag of pointe shoes into my hands, which I threw on the floor. I looked him up and down and couldn't believe what I was seeing.

My name was written all over his t-shirt and down the legs of his trousers. He had written, 'I love you, Monica and I want to get back together.' He had two love hearts drawn on his bum with 'Monica Loughman' written between them. I struggled to find the Russian words I needed.

'Do you think I'm yours? I am not a doll! You can't do this to me. You're not my friend anymore.'

'No, I love you,' he said and his face crumbled.

'Give me your shirt,' I answered, ignoring his hurt expression.

'*Nyet!*'

'Give it to me!' I shouted. 'I'll give you a t-shirt to walk around in.'

He just stood there grinning from ear to ear. He had no intentions of budging and he didn't seem to care that I was visibly upset. I started pushing him and screaming at him in English.

'Give me the bloody t-shirt! It's my name—not yours!' I was shaking with anger by now and I was ready to physically rip it off him. He realised how serious I was and he knew that any chance he ever had of getting back with me was quickly diminishing. He reluctantly took his t-shirt off.

'How dare you treat me like this?' I screamed at him in English, and I threw him a shirt and told him to put it on.

'We're not talking about this again,' I hissed and I left the room without looking back.

Ballet class started the following day and I stood at the side barre with all the tall girls waiting for Ulanova to arrive. Emma stood on the opposite side with the smaller girls. All of the Russian girls in the class were graduating that year so they were about 18-years-old. I was the youngest and I hoped I wouldn't be out of my depth.

The class went well and without any incidents, but the Russian girls weren't very friendly. That didn't matter. I was still delighted to be in class with them, however, because I felt they were on par with the professional dancers.

The next day I went back to my place at the side barre and Ulanova came up and took me by the hand. I was quite worried because I was sure I wasn't good enough. I thought she was going to bring me to a younger class, but she brought me to the middle of the back barre, where I was suddenly in the most coveted spot in the room.

I could see the Russian girls' eyes widen with shock. If looks could kill, I would have died on the spot. It made me a little bit nervous that I was making enemies before I even had a chance to talk to them, but I soon learned to ignore the looks and concentrate on the combinations.

When we came off the barre I was up at the front of the class and this couldn't have been much better for learning.

In another sense though, it couldn't have been much worse because the Russians hated me for it. I was a foreigner who wasn't even graduating that year, yet I was given the prime position.

The Russians have a very unique style of teaching ballet. They regularly called us fat cows. The teachers would call me a fool, an idiot, or thick. Out of nowhere you'd get a belt in your back, in your knee or foot, or a kick on the backside. Most ballet teachers hit us but not to the point of bruising. They did it to all the students and we accepted it without question. Most of them balanced it correctly with praise, so it didn't make me feel bad. It was better to be hit than be ignored.

Ulanova conducted her classes in this manner. She made me feel like I was not doing my best and I could do a thousand times better. She often called me stupid but she also went out of her way to make me feel good about myself. She would also get me to show combinations to the class.

'Oh, look,' she'd say. 'Monica can do this. Do it for them.'

I'd have to do the combination by myself and all the other girls would be throwing dirty looks at me. It was difficult to get used to another teacher's style, as

Svetlana hadn't been physical with us, but I soon got used to Ulanova and accepted the blows.

We started duet (pas de deux) classes in second year, which meant we were dancing with boys for the first time. The Russian girls and boys had done duet for the two years prior to this, so we had a lot of catching up to do.

I was very excited about duet because we were getting a step closer to becoming professional dancers. We would be learning pas de deux for the first time. We all gathered in the classroom waiting for the teacher to arrive, when Ulanova came in and told us that she was separating the class. She said that anyone who weighed over 50kgs wouldn't be allowed to participate, as it was too much of a strain on the boys. She appeared uncomfortable saying this and I got the impression that she had been sent on someone's behalf to do the dirty work. She asked a number of girls to get weighed after class.

The boys came into the classroom at the same time as the teacher and they just stood there grinning at us. Sakharova's son, Alexandr Sakharov, was our teacher. He was about 36 years of age and was small with curly hair.

My first impression of him was that he really didn't want to be there. He told the boys to pick out their partners while he sat on the bench in a disinterested manner.

One of the boys stood out from the others; he was tall and muscular with black wavy hair and had the most fabulous chiselled face. He pulled a Russian girl, Anya, towards him and then turned his striking blue eyes towards me and held out his hand. I went weak at the knees as I looked up at him. He was the most beautiful boy I had ever seen. His name was Maxim.

I later discovered he had always danced with Anya and she was one of the best in the class. She was small, agile, and extremely well co-ordinated. We had to share him as a partner, as there weren't enough boys to go around.

We took turns dancing with the boys and Anya went first. She started doing small jumps and lifts with Maxim, which gave me time to watch and learn. The lifts looked fairly simple, as they didn't go above the shoulder. It mainly involved running, jumping, and catching.

I couldn't wait for my turn. I secretly hoped that Anya would fall and have to leave the class so I could dance with Maxim. As I stood there, I noticed that most of the girls stared at Maxim dancing. He had a magnetic quality to him that drew everyone in. I also noticed that I was getting dirty looks for the second day in a row.

There was one unfortunate girl in the class who was extremely awkward and constantly kneed her partner in the groin. Every time this girl lifted her leg she seemed to injure her partner; needless to say, nobody wanted to dance with her after that.

The whole class just fell around laughing when it happened, although it is a fact of life in ballet that at some point the male dancers gets kicked in the groin; it's inevitable.

Before I knew it, we swapped partners and I was in Maxim's capable hands. I got through the first class without any incidents. By the end of the class though, most of the boys hobbled out as they had been kicked and beaten in some way or another.

I seemed to impress Maxim in duet and we danced very well together. We spent a lot of the class joking and giggling and it was obvious to everyone that we had a crush on each other. We always found an excuse to grab a hold of each other and practise the lifts.

I always hated when Maxim had to dance with Anya because she could talk to him when they would be standing together, and she always tried to monopolise him.

She fancied him too so there was great competition between us. She was part of the first group, which got to practise for longer periods with the boys. I would be standing at the barre waiting for them to finish, wishing the floor would swallow Anya up. It was that simple.

Every girl that was waiting on her turn was feeling that way, because we hated being second best.

It wasn't necessarily that everyone felt attracted to the boys. Nobody wanted to stand around because it was such a fun class. If Anya was out sick I would go first, but I never had Maxim to myself for a whole class because some boys had three girls to dance with.

I remember that class for several reasons. After a few weeks we found out that our teacher didn't bother turning up whenever he had a hangover. He was the artistic director's son and could do whatever he liked. He taught the boys' ballet class, so they were very familiar with his behaviour, but I couldn't get used to it. If he didn't show up, we had to leave after 15 minutes. In a normal ballet class, our pianist would play the music and we would do class on our own but it was considered too dangerous to do lifts without a teacher present.

At the start of the year, Donna and I had a bet to see who could wear their soft pointe shoes the longest. We normally ended up changing our shoes every three weeks, but we thought it would be funny to see how long they could last.

The leather on the shoe would wear down very quickly even though we darned the shoes every night.

We hadn't been able to get our hands on white thread, however, so we ended up using olive green thread to darn the pink satin to the leather.

After three weeks the satin turned brown and the shoes stank of glue, leather, and sweat, but we persevered. I darned my initials into the heel of the shoe and roses where the ball of my foot fell.

Every night we'd sit and darn them even though the shoes would be thoroughly soggy from the water and the sweat. After about 10 weeks my shoes had been darned so often they were about two sizes bigger than they should be. They also weighed about a pound more.

When I put them on the radiator to dry at night they became rock solid and I had to break them in every morning. At that stage I had been wearing them for about five months and I was determined to beat Donna. I went into class and was warming up at the barre, when Tatyana, the pianist came over. She told me that my shoes were a disgrace and that it was disrespectful to Ulanova to come to class like that. I looked down at my feet and agreed with her at once. The shoes were now brown, with olive green embroidery all over them and bore no resemblance to the other girls baby pink satin shoes. The following day I came in with new pointe shoes: Donna had won the bet.

After a few weeks of classes I saw Donna standing outside her classroom looking upset. She started ranting the minute she saw me because she had been asked to leave her duet class.

The school enforced a blanket policy of banning girls that weighed over 50kgs from practising duet. This was unfair. It was biased towards the smaller girls as tall people obviously weigh more.

Donna only weighed eight stone and was about 5'10" so she was physically perfect. It was outrageous to suggest otherwise. She was genuinely upset and I could see why she was lashing out. It was a humiliating experience.

From now on she would have to get a slip from the doctor every week to say how much she weighed indicating whether she had lost weight or not. There was no formal support system there for the girls that had problems with their weight. All of these girls were under 18 years of age. They should have had someone telling them how to lose weight sensibly and how to keep it off, but instead there was a culture of crash dieting and one or two of the Russian girls even developed eating disorders. There was a girl in my class called Svetlana who stopped eating completely when she discovered she weighed too much for duet. She just drank liquids. She was a very talented young girl, but she had big muscular thighs. She was fanatical about her body and was constantly trying to build up her muscles, which made her heavier and chunky. She gradually got to the stage where she had big legs but no waist and you could see the veins through her skin.

She was lucky because Ulanova recognised that she had an eating disorder. She took her under her wing and ensured that Svetlana started eating again. She used to wake her up every morning, make her get dressed, and bring her by the hand to her apartment. Ulanova lived in the building next to the Internat and she gave Svetlana breakfast there every day and sat with her for 30 minutes afterwards to make sure she digested it. Then she would let her go to class.

Somebody would sit with her during lunch to make sure she ate and digested her lunch. Ulanova would go into the canteen to ensure this and she personally saw to it that Svetlana broke her eating disorder and got back into a habit of eating two proper meals a day. Very gradually Svetlana started to put on weight and because she had starved herself, the weight piled on very quickly. The school turned a blind eye to this, however, as they felt partly responsible for her eating disorder and she never was sent to be weighed again.

By the end of the year she seemed to have regained control over her eating and her weight was at a reasonable level again, but we were all very aware of the damage she had done to herself through a few months of starvation. Her natural metabolism was out of sync and she had a weight problem for years after that. She continued in ballet, however, and joined a company after graduating that year.

The girls who weren't allowed to participate in the class weren't even allowed into the classroom to watch. They would be bullied out by Sakharova. She would come into the classroom every now and then and check our weight. We had to stand with our hands by our side while she would come up and literally stare at our bodies. We were at the age where we were already self-conscious, so you could say it destroyed our confidence.

She would walk up to one of the girls, thump her and call her a fat cow. She would grab any flesh she could and verbally abuse us. One of her favourite places to check for excess fat was between our shoulder blades. If she could pinch more than an inch, then she would kick you out, and you wouldn't get back into class until you weighed 49kgs.

In those circumstances it wasn't enough to weigh 50kgs. At 50kgs you weren't even allowed to step into the room. Having said all that, she made exceptions for a few people who were in her ballet class and let them participate in duet.

None of the Irish girls developed an eating disorder, though there was constant pressure to be thin. Within each class the girls were divided by their physique. The tall girls would take one side barre and as they got further back, they got fatter. It was the same on the other side. The back barre, as I said, was reserved for the best in the class, who also happened to be the thinnest.

One night Donna and I felt very homesick and we sat in our room chatting. We upset each other talking about home and we both ended up crying.

I was sitting on the ground bawling my eyes out when Lidiya, one of the *Mamoushkas* barged into our room.

'Oh! Are you okay?' she asked, when she saw that I was crying.

'Yeah,' I replied. 'I just want to go home. I miss my family.'

'Don't worry. It won't be long before you see them,' she smiled.

I made some coffee and forgot all about the *Mamoushka's* brief appearance. The next day I went into my Russian class and the teacher, Elena, pulled me aside.

'You were drunk last night, weren't you?'

'No,' I replied feeling confused.

'Lidiya said you were lying on the floor, drunk out of your mind.'

'What?'

'Yes. You're going to be taken up over this. You could be thrown out.'

'Hold on a second,' I said, and my voice started to rise. 'Come on. I'm sorting this out now.'

I knew being drunk was looked upon very seriously by the school. I wanted to put a stop to this before the rumour took hold. I was shaking. I couldn't understand why the *Mamoushka* would say something like that. There was no drink in the room.

There was no smell of alcohol in the room, and even worse, I was still on the pledge and I hadn't touched alcohol in my life.

Elena and I left the class and we went into our assistant director's office. Although I was as timid as a mouse around authority, I was so angry that I didn't consider what the correct protocol might be. I was enraged that Lidiya had damaged my reputation without reason or merit. I could have been expelled and my future was on the line.

As soon as Pidemskaya called us in I launched into a defence.

'How dare she say that!' I said. 'I was not drunk. You cannot prove it, but I am willing to give a blood test to prove that I had no alcohol in me.'

'You were drunk,' Pidemskaya drawled lazily, as if she didn't really care. 'You were crying from the drink.'

'I was not! Ask Donna, ask anyone! Root through the bins; do whatever you have to do. That's not fair and I'm not having it. I was crying because I was feeling homesick. Since when am I not allowed to cry?

You can't go around accusing people of this based on someone crying.'

I was so indignant that Pidemskaya started to believe me. She knew I respected her authority and I would never speak to her like this unless I was innocent. She saw I was so riled I was willing to do anything. I felt that I had nothing to lose. She asked Elena to bring the *Mamoushka* into the room. I stared at Lidiya in disbelief when she came in. I looked at her and waited for her to say something. She appeared very uncomfortable and didn't know where to look.

'I must have got the wrong end of the story. I mustn't have understood. I thought you said you were drunk.'

'I don't even drink. That's no excuse to do that to someone.'

Pidemskaya seemed to have had enough of the conversation at this point and told me to forget about it and go back to class. I left without receiving an apology and I felt that it hadn't been resolved properly.

I didn't get on with Pidemskaya after that. Although I hadn't challenged her authority directly, I went in there in a rage, and nobody loses their temper with their elders in Russia. I was shouting, but it wasn't meant to be directed towards her. However, there was no love lost between us since that day.

I threw myself into my school work, although I wasn't doing well in character class at all. I started to skip classes once again. Our character teacher this year was a young tall woman who had been a principal dancer in the Perm Theatre, but she fell into the orchestra pit during a performance and broke her back.

The doctors put steel pins into her spine, so she could walk with a hobble, but she was never able to dance after that. She was a lovely woman, but a really boring teacher.

I turned up at the beginning of the year to discover that the boys were also in this class. I had always danced the male role prior to this, so I had no idea how to do the girl's steps. I was so bad at it, and I hated being terrible—especially in front of the boys. The other girls were fabulous at it and they were having great fun. They flicked their skirts and moved in a sultry and confident way. I felt like a two-legged donkey beside them.

I kept messing up my steps, so I was too embarrassed to go back in.

Emma was very good at character and when I missed a class I would ask her to show me what they had done that day and she would always show me the steps when I asked.

It made it harder for me to go back in though because I realised I was completely out of the loop. I thought I'd never catch up.

I had decided I was going to work harder than ever in ballet that year, so I went over to the studio to practise every night. I was keeping up with the class and feeling happy, however, the competitive environment spilled over into everything else. In Perm, bullying and intimidation was rife. It confronted you no matter what you did. Ballet can cause terrible jealously.

One day in class I was kicked in the bum by a girl called Veronika. I didn't know what to do and I didn't know why she was doing it. I had noticed that she was giving me dirty looks when I was dancing with Maxim, but I couldn't imagine that she was kicking me because of that. I got through the class with just a few more kicks.

This set the tone for the year. I was consistently kicked on the wrist, on the legs, the arms, the bum—anywhere that she and her friends could reach. When these particular girls would water the floor I'd find that I'd be standing in a puddle of water.

I still couldn't converse with Maxim properly but if we were ever caught standing together trying to talk, the bullying would get much worse.

Veronika was giving me such a hard time. When I'd walk into the class she'd cough and say '*suka*', not really hiding the fact that she was calling me a bitch. In the middle of class she'd hit me. Some of her close friends were calling me names, and it was all over Maxim.

But Veronika wasn't the only one who had a problem with Maxim. After a school disco, Maxim and I were sitting on the stairs outside my Russian classroom chatting. Maxim was leaning close to me and I was so caught up in the moment that I didn't notice Gonserique walking towards us. He called Maxim over, insisting they needed to talk.

I couldn't quite make out what they were saying, but after a few minutes they were shouting at each other. They disappeared around the corner and I could hear them pushing and shoving each other. I sat there wondering what to do. I was worried but I must admit that part of me felt a perverse thrill that these two very fit boys were fighting over a skinny Irish girl, who couldn't even talk to them properly.

Suddenly I heard the sound of shattering glass and I ran down the hall to see what had happened. Maxim was standing in a pile of glass and Gonserique was nowhere to be seen.

Maxim took me by the hand and explained that Gonserique had thrown a bottle at him but had hit the glass door instead. As he told me what happened, Gonserique reappeared and said that he needed to talk to Maxim again, but this time Gonserique was apologetic.

They went off to resolve their differences and I was left to walk home on my own.

Chapter Eight

While I didn't care about my friendship with Gonserique, I did care about my friendship with Donna, which began to flounder around this time. The school put us all under pressure in different ways, though we were all under huge pressure to maintain our weight. Ballet dancers are supposed to look good and this expectation starts in the schools.

I wasn't having an easy time. I was physically bullied and kicked by Veronika in ballet class; this had a detrimental effect on my moods. Donna had her own problems and as a consequence we fought all the time. We were unable to give each other the help we needed.

I was fanatical about cleanliness that particular year and I strove to keep our room spotless, whereas Donna would step out of her clothes and leave them where they landed. We constantly fell out because the room seemed to be in a shambles.

It's funny the things that can annoy you when you're a hormonal teenager. Donna used to leave the light on at night, which prevented me from sleeping.

After about six weeks into the term I knew it had been a mistake to move in with her. We were spending more time arguing than having fun. We just seemed to drive each other mad.

The bullying I received at Veronika's hands effected me personally. I wanted Donna to support and protect me like a parent, but she was only a teenager and she couldn't. She was desperately unhappy with the way she was treated in duet and she simply couldn't offer me the support I needed. She was also under pressure, albeit of a different type.

She started spending more time with James and Emma. After two months of living together, any time I came into the room Donna would be gone. I spent the evenings on my own either darning my shoes or reading.

James, Donna, and Emma started going to the hotel down the road where some of the ballet dancers from the theatre lived and they would occasionally attend parties there.

The demise of my relationship with Donna built up very gradually and I didn't really see it happening. I was so focused on ballet and duet that I didn't notice we were slowly speaking less and less. At that time, I was so competitive that I used to sneak over to the studio at night to practise. I often lied about where I was going. I'd say I was washing my laundry or something. I'm sure this didn't help our relationship. I would come in after practising in the studio at night and wonder where Donna was and if she was okay.

Other things also irritated me, though perhaps I also overreacted to certain events. Sometimes Donna would borrow my clothes and she would wear them before I got a chance to. I might have been saving some new clothes for a special occasion, but when she would ask to borrow them I felt that I couldn't say no. This was the type of row that teenage sisters would normally have.

I'm sure I did lots of other things that made Donna angry, but we never fell out for too long. We ended up being friends again. My defence mechanism was to work twice as hard as everyone else. Anytime I had a row with someone, it just made me determined to be more successful.

Myself and Donna decided it would be better if we didn't live together anymore, following one of our rows. This was a big deal at the time and we were both upset, but looking back on it now, it really was trivial and melodramatic. I had become friendly with one of the other Irish girls, Gillian, and we decided to move in together.

I was happier with my living arrangements, and that made everything much easier to deal with. Gillian was a very relaxed girl and we would go over to the studio together in the evenings. I remained very bitter about the whole row, and I was frequently in a bad mood. I didn't notice that I was giving out about Veronika and Donna the whole time until Gillian said it to me one day.

'You know Monica. You've turned into everything you once gave out about. You're negative the whole time and you constantly give out about people. You'd want to cop onto yourself!'

I was stunned. I didn't realise what I was doing, but as soon as she said it, I knew she was right. The truth was that I missed Donna and I missed being her friend.

After about two months of not talking to Donna, I bumped into her in the hall outside our rooms. I decided to bite the bullet and see if we could start talking again.

Luckily Donna also wanted to make friends, so we sat down and talked about what happened between us. We had a laugh and ended up becoming the best of friends again.

This was the turning point of the year for me. Things were finally looking up and once I felt that I had a group of friends around me, I felt strong enough to take Veronika on. She had been playing mind games and bullying me all year, and now it was time for it to stop.

I got all the Irish to stand together outside of class when she was on her own and I pointed at her and started laughing. I wasn't actually saying anything about her, but it intimidated her. She wasn't so cool and brave when she was on her own, and after a few more incidents of this kind, she stopped bothering me in class. I was aware that I was treating her in a similar manner to the way she had treated me, but I thought she needed a taste of her own medicine. Her friends also backed off as they saw that I was just trying to get on in school, and I didn't respond to their kicks.

A lot of love affairs and crushes happened during duet that year. It is absolutely necessary to trust your dance partner completely, thus, it is easy to develop a fondness for that person. Claire was partnered with Maxim's best friend, Sasha, and it was obvious by the way he looked at her that he was crazy about her.

Sasha became so infatuated with Claire that every time he had a drink he would try to climb up the drain pipes to the bathroom on the third floor. Claire wasn't interested in him and tried to talk him into going back to his apartment before the *Mamoushkas* discovered him hanging around.

One night before Easter, James was on the phone when he heard a crash outside the window. He ran out to discover Sasha lying intoxicated in the snow, laughing uncontrollably. James heard Claire and I shouting down from the third floor.

'Are you okay?'

'He's grand, don't worry,' James shouted back and made sure that Sasha was alright, before leaving him to his own devices. The following morning, Sasha came into school with his ankle bandaged and a sheepish grin. He finally got the message that Claire wasn't interested in him, but he was unable to dance until his ankle healed at the end of the year.

After Easter, we went on a three-night mini tour. We went to a town called Kirovo-Chepetsk, which is a ten-hour train journey from Perm. It's located between Perm and Moscow.

Claire's room-mate, Natasha, was from Kirovo-Chepetsk and was hand-picked by Sakharova to become the next prima ballerina. She had graduated the previous year, but Sakharova asked her to stay on so she could groom her for competitions. Natasha was about 5'3" with fabulous long legs, and waist-length black hair. She had a perfectly symmetrical face with deep brown eyes and had a lovely gentle nature.

There are several routes to becoming a prima ballerina. Some people take years and gradually work their way up the ranks from the corps de ballet to principal. In Russia, the government can proclaim someone to be a prima. A theatre can highly recommend a ballerina and a committee is sent out to watch her perform. If she impresses them sufficiently she receives prima status.

There are also certain competitions that a ballerina can win to become a prima, such as the Concourse, or the Moscow International Ballet Competition.

A prima has to be able to dance any role given to her. Her scope and technical abilities must range from an easier principal role such as the sylph in *La Sylphide* to the more intricate and demanding roles from choreographers Balanchine and Petipa. There are only a handful of prima ballerinas in Russia and it can take years to achieve this coveted title.

Natasha was the focal point of the show and the locals turned out in droves to support her and the school. It was a very exciting time for us.

Ulanova, Bystritskaya, and Pidemskaya accompanied us on the trip. The Irish students had to stay with Russian families, while the Russian students stayed in a hostel. We weren't allowed to mix with them because we were considered a bad influence, even though everyone seemed to be having a smashing time without us.

I shared a room with Donna and Anna and we were raging because we had to live with an old couple. We were offloaded early but at least we had the luxury of a toilet and showers. The Russians had one toilet and one shower between the whole lot of them.

I was dancing in the corps of *Swan Lake* and I was excited to be performing in front of a Russian audience. We all came on stage for our part, and stood in two parallel lines.

There's a gap in the middle of the swans, where the swan queen, Odette, comes on and runs through looking for her prince.

The swan queen and the prince were both in the graduation year in our school and I didn't know them very well, but I knew they were a couple.

Odette has a dance where she's by herself for about a minute and the music hits this big crescendo when her prince is supposed to come out . . . but he didn't appear.

The girl who was dancing the swan queen, Veronika, turned around and I heard just one word come out of her mouth—'shit!'

She kept on dancing, making it up as she went along. This was at the start of an adagio so the music is slow and tapered. It was impossible for her to make any sense of it by herself. The audience started to giggle softly because the Russians know their ballet, and they knew what was supposed to happen. She kept dancing towards the wings and screaming into them, 'Where are you, you bastard? Yevgeny! Someone call him.'

There was a full conversation taking place on stage.

We were visibly shaking with laughter. It was impossible to keep a straight face.

Halfway through the adagio Yevgeny ran out onto the stage in his stockinged feet. He was in such a panic that he had forgotten to put on his shoes. His big toes were sticking out through his tights. His jacket was half undone and his hair was a mess. He had been playing poker and forgotten his entry, and when he was dragged up to the stage, he had no time to fix himself.

He was so confused he didn't know where to start. The adagio lasts for about seven minutes and Veronika had already danced by herself for about three or four minutes prior to this. When he came out on stage all hell broke loose. She kept on 'accidently on purpose' kicking him. All you could hear was 'Ugh!'

The audience loved it and went wild in their applause. Normally when the principal couple take their bow, the man brings the woman forward, but when Yevgeny went to bring Veronika to the front, she turned around and walked off and he was left standing there gobsmacked. He salvaged it, however, by doing a port de bras, and then hobbled off the stage.

The audience realised we were kids, so they saw the funny side of it. Needless to say, the swan queen and the prince's romance ended that night.

Chapter Nine

Coming up to the final exams I was under immense pressure to do well. I had to reach the same standard that the graduation students had attained. This effectively meant cramming eight years of tuition into two years.

The year had gone well and I felt that I had improved in leaps and bounds. Ulanova still singled me out for attention and the Russian girls had finally accepted me as a part of their class.

Two weeks before the exam, Ulanova went around the classroom telling the girls whether they needed to lose weight or not. I was confident that I was fine, as my weight had never been an issue. But I got the shock of my life when she smiled and told me to lose three kilos before the exam. I looked at her blankly wondering why the hell she hadn't given me more notice.

I was horrified and immediately changed my eating habits. I only drank coffee and ate dry breakfast cereal for the next two weeks. I also took up smoking to curb my appetite. My only indulgence was to drink a can of Pepsi and eat a handful of cereal before every class, to give me enough energy to get through it.

Now it was time to concentrate on the exams. I was toiling through piano without much success, and I was so unhappy in character class. I had such a mental block that I couldn't even remember the steps. I was sure I was going to fail this subject, but I ended up struggling through it.

Four weeks before the exams, I was paired with Maxim's friend, Sasha, for duet. Sasha was taller than Maxim, but he wasn't as good as him. We did well in the exam, but I would have preferred to have Maxim as a partner. This was one exam that I really enjoyed and I wasn't surprised that the majority of the class received a 5.

The ballet exam couldn't have gone better. The barre work went without a glitch and I jumped higher than everyone else when we moved onto the floor. I left the exam feeling on top of the world. I knew this was the best class I had done since I joined the school.

Ulanova seemed really pleased. She gave everyone a hug and scuttled off to see what marks we got. All the girls were delighted with themselves for doing so well. Everyone in the school was allowed to watch the exams, if they could fit in the door. The whole side of the room was filled with younger students, who anxiously watched our every move. It was great to have the support, but I was also mindful about the possibility of messing up in front of my peers.

As I came down the stairs to get my results Anya and Xenia, who had stayed in my house in Ireland, ran up to me. 'You got a 5!'

'I did not!'

'You did! You did!' and they proceeded to name out all the people who had gotten a 5.

I made my way over to the board and I met Ulanova coming in my direction to give us our results. She held my hand and gave me a big kiss.

'Well done! I didn't think you could do that well. Even I am surprised. I didn't see that in you the whole year.'

Veronika got a 4 so she was disgusted. Everyone was hugging and kissing and anyone that got a 5 was crying. It was very emotional. It was the end of eight years of study for the Russians.

While this was going on Donna and Anna's exam had begun. I went over to the Internat to relax and get changed. James came over and told me that a few of the Russian girls didn't receive a mark in their ballet exam because of their weight. I was astounded but also angry on their behalf. It didn't matter how good they were. If they weren't thin, they would never be considered good enough. This illustrated the importance the school placed on appearances; if a girl was over eight stone, they refused to mark her in the exam.

I went over to the school to see how Donna had performed, and I was delighted to hear she also had received a 5. The following day, Donna excelled in her character exam. I got goosebumps just watching her, while unfortunately, I just about trundled through mine.

We normally finished school in June, but we had to come home early, because we had an audition for the Arts Council. We had all applied for a grant, which we had to audition for. We paid our teacher $10 each for extra tuition to get variations from a ballet ready; we worked extremely hard on them.

After the excitement of my performance in Russia, I was confident I would impress the Irish panel. I turned up to the audition brimming with confidence.

We started by doing a short ballet class, while they sat behind a large desk and took notes.

We were then asked to perform our individual variations and we began to put our pointe shoes on. One of the panel told us to continue wearing our soft shoes, as the floor was too slippy for pointes. I was happy to dance in either shoe type and when I finished I knew my performance had been as good as the Russians.

After the variation I was asked to take a seat in front of the panel for the final stage of the audition, where I was questioned. It went downhill from there. They told me I was very thin. The questioning continued along this vein, but it felt more like an interrogation. They said they didn't like the Russian style; they asked where I saw myself in the future. I was a teenager. I hadn't a clue where life was going to bring me.

I was very upset and as soon as I left the room I was in tears. I couldn't understand why they were so aggressive when I was doing so well. I finished top of the class. I knew the variation I had performed was good, because the other students who had seen my exam told me I'd done a brilliant job.

When I told my Dad the questions I had been asked, he rang the Arts Council and complained.

A few days later a letter arrived in the post. I could see from the postmark that it was from the Arts Council, so I called Dad and we opened it together.

It stated that they were unable to give me funding, but I noticed the date on the letter was April, but I didn't do the audition until June.

I was infuriated. I had come home early to do this audition and had paid teachers to give me extra tuition.

I rang Donna and found that she had received an identical letter with the same date. Dad phoned the Arts Council once again.

'Do you realise how upset these children are? You brought them home a week early to do an audition that was meaningless. What are you doing?'

After much to-ing and fro-ing, everyone who had received this letter got a cheque for £300. That was my very first run-in with the Arts Council and I never got a penny from them after that. I felt that they told me to my face that I wasn't good enough to receive State funding.

Their attitude made me lose faith in adults. I was bitterly disappointed. We had worked extremely hard; we worked as hard as the other people in the arts; yet we weren't being acknowledged and classical ballet wasn't recognised in our own country.

The weekend after the audition we were performing in a Russian/Irish Gala with the Russian students in the National Concert Hall in Dublin and in University Concert Hall, Limerick. I did the second variation from the pas de trois from Swan Lake.

Ulanova had made something of me from nothing. All I needed was a bit more coaching. She had polished the variation so much that it was practically perfect. I danced it in the theatre as a professional, and I always danced it the way I remember learning it in school.

While the shows had gone well, my private life was about to take a turn for the worse. It soon became very obvious that Maxim wasn't even smiling at me. I went up to him after the last show and asked him what was wrong.

'You won't even say hello to me. What's wrong with you?'

'Get away from me,' he scowled.

'What have I done? Talk to me; tell me.'

He just turned around and said, 'I don't want to have anything to do with you anymore.' If you could hear someone's heart breaking, that would have been the moment you heard mine. I just stood there and watched him walk away from me. He was trying to tell me in simple Russian to get lost.

When we got on the bus I was devastated but I kept my cool. Maxim's friend Sasha came and sat beside me. He put his arm around me and asked if I was okay. I told him what had happened.

'Sure I'll be grand. Life goes on.'

Four years later when I had finished school I found out what had happened. James told me one night when we were having a drink in Dublin, that Sasha had told Maxim it wasn't just him I was flirting with. Sasha said I also had a crush on him.

I was able to laugh about it by then. Sasha was manipulating the situation the whole time. Sasha told Maxim that I was throwing myself at him, and because he sat beside me on the bus, it looked as if we were together.

Maxim joined the Perm Theatre after graduating that year and I never stepped foot in the theatre while he was there. Later he became a soloist in the Kirov Theatre in St. Petersburg.

Chapter Ten

As was becoming a pattern, some of the girls that had been in Perm the previous year didn't return. Gillian, Darina, Emily and Antonia stayed in Ireland while Claire decided to go to London.

Again, a few new students joined us. Lucy Hickey and Harriet Parsons had been in Perm the year before I joined. They stayed at home for two years to do their Leaving Certificate and came back for my third year. Two girls named Karen O'Neill and Jane Mangan joined the school that year.

The year began quite smoothly. During the summer, Donna and I agreed to share a room again, so when the mini bus pulled up outside the Internat, I ran quickly to the third floor to secure Claire's old room. It was the biggest and the best on the floor. The main source of excitement as we bustled around our rooms was the fact that one of us was going to be in Madame Sakharova's class. Although we knew she was a very tough teacher, it was still considered an honour and a privilege to be invited to train under her. She handpicked the best girls and had a reputation for creating world-class ballerinas.

Everyone gathered in our room and we sat on the beds chatting, waiting for John Baraldi to advise us on which teacher we would have. It wasn't long before he appeared. He didn't mince his words.

'I was talking to Madame Sakharova and Monica and Anna are going into her class this year.' I was elated when I heard my name mentioned. 'Harriet, Donna, Emma and Lucy—you're all in Svetlana Ivanova's class.'

Karen and Jane were put into a class with the younger Russian girls, while James and Gavin had one of the male teachers.

The other girls were delighted to be in Svetlana's class once again as she had been great in first year.

The following morning Anna and I went into class and Sakharova placed us at the barre. Once again I was put in the middle of the back barre but I wasn't happy about this as I knew Sakharova wouldn't leave me alone for a minute. She was the only teacher who actually scared me. After she put us on the barre, she left the classroom. She always had to be in a million places at the same time because she was the artistic director of the school as well as the principal. The pianist played for us and Sakharova's granddaughter, Dasha, who was a student in the class, started giving out instructions.

Sakharova returned after about ten minutes and continued giving the rest of the class. She came over to me and started trying to explain what she wanted me to do.

'Lift your leg 45 degrees,' she said, although she was pointing at a 90 degree angle.

I looked at her hand and said, 'Okay.' I didn't know whether to follow her verbal instruction or her hand gesture, so I raised my leg to 90 degrees, where she had pointed.

She hit my leg and brought it down to 45 degrees and said, 'No! This is 90 degrees.'

I was completely confused by now. I didn't know what she wanted. There was no explanation for where this was coming from and I didn't know what to do. For Sakharova there didn't need to be an explanation. She had everything confused in her mind.

She went over to Anna and started talking to her. Sakharova was looking at her and trying to be very calm, but Anna couldn't do what she wanted.

Sakharova came over and poked me in the side and told me to show Anna what to do. I explained to Anna what I thought Sakharova wanted. I didn't want the woman to be riled.

This got to be a pattern in the class. I was on the back barre and Anna was on the side barre and I would have to call over to her to explain. If Anna didn't get it I would be thinking, 'Anna, please, come on, you know it.' The first class wasn't too bad though and we were sort of happy with how it went. John was leaving for Ireland that evening and I met him to wish him a safe journey back. 'How was Sakharova's class?' he asked, knowing that she had a reputation as a strict teacher.

'It went really well,' I replied, not entirely sure I meant it. I didn't tell him how nervous I was. 'We enjoyed it.'

I was quite apprehensive about what lay ahead. I suspected it would be a difficult year, because we had such high expectations of the class, but I told myself that everything would be grand.

We returned to class the following morning and it started to get worse. Sakharova started hitting me for stupid things. She asked us to do a ronde de jambe at the barre but she made us put our backs to the barre while we held onto it with both hands. We stood with our leg at 90 degrees while standing on demi-pointe for about ten minutes. It was totally unnatural and didn't make sense. I thought I was going to cry because I felt like I was in hell.

I wasn't learning anything; I was just completely drained from her ludicrous demands.

She came up and talked to us when we were doing this and if she couldn't see the sweat running off us, we were in trouble. I was lucky; I sweated really easily so it was obvious I was working hard. There was one girl who didn't sweat, though, and Sakharova was constantly over at her asking, 'Why aren't you sweating, you fat cow?'

The classes continued along this vein. She would come over and kick me underneath my thigh if she wasn't happy with my position. I would keep my eyes down and hope she would stop. There were only ten of us in her class, so it was really personal and very intense. There were two other foreign girls in the class. They were Japanese and the rest were Russian.

We stayed on the barre for the first few days and then we moved into the centre of the room. She paired Dasha and I together. We were exactly the same age— our birthdays were even the same month. Dasha was very well-known in Russia at that time because she was a child star.

We started dancing but Sakharova didn't seem happy with anything I did and we were made do things over and over again. Dasha was getting really pissed off and I could hear her giving out stink about me. Between her and her grandmother, it was coming at me from all directions and because there was so few of us in the class; there was nowhere to hide.

The class was supposed to be 90 minutes long, but it could last anything up to two and a half hours. It depended on what mood Sakharova was in. You never knew what she was going to come up with. She could make us stand at the barre for two hours and we would be absolutely wrecked. I was so tired after these classes that I didn't even know where I was going to get the strength to get out of bed the next day.

We weren't allowed leave the classroom without getting fully dressed. Sakharova made us wear lots of clothes. We had to wear a top with a hood, or have a towel over our head and then have something warm wrapped around our necks. Then we would curtsy and she would leave the room. Afterwards all the girls would stand around like zombies for ages going, 'Thank God that's over.'

I was visibly shaken after a particularly difficult class and Polina, one of the students in the class, came over and asked if I was okay.

'What can I do to stop her hitting me?' I asked. 'What's wrong with me?'

'Don't look into her eyes. She hates that. Stand with your hands behind your back and let her talk to you without flinching,' Polina advised. 'If you try not to draw attention to yourself, hopefully she'll leave you alone and get on with the class.'

I thanked Polina for her help and wandered away from the class. After any of Sakharova's classes, when I would be walking down the corridor, people would be saying hello to me, but I wouldn't really be with it. At the end of the class, we would be like old women shuffling out of the room. Everyone knew we were her dancers because of the way we walked.

Sakharova always came in wearing woolly jumpers, polo necks, and leggings. She was a bizarre looking woman.

The other teachers wore shoes into class, but she wore her own slippers; they were sort of pointy. After attending her class for a week, I got to know what kind of humour she was in by the clothes she wore that day. The brighter they were, the mellower she would be. If her outfit was coordinated, she was in an even better mood. If it looked like she got dressed in the dark you knew you were in for a bad day.

There is a culture of physical correction in Russian schools. If a teacher hits you, it means they're paying attention to you. Other teachers, such as Ulanova, had the balance right, but Sakharova started getting really violent.

I didn't know what to do. She gradually got more aggressive and vicious towards me. She usually started after the warm up. She would come up and give me a dig in the back and then she would start screaming in my face. I would have to stop what I was doing and just stand there without moving. The whole class had to stand with their hands by their sides when this happened, but this could go on for half an hour. We were often standing around for a lot of the class. In her earlier days, she had a reputation for being a great teacher, but I think the stress got to her.

I remember I was talking to some of the Russian students after one of the classes and they told me not to cry during class, no matter what happened. She hated it when students cried and she kicked them out.

One particular day she was hitting and kicking me. We had only started the second combination on the barre when she came up and hit me on the side of the face. She stood in front of me and said, 'What are you doing, you stupid fat cow?'

I just stood there and she started walking closer to me, so I stepped backwards. She kept on invading my space and walking almost on top of me, so I kept walking back further and further. The girls were walking away from the barre because I was backing into them. Although Polina told me not to look her in the eye I did it deliberately that day. She's only 5 foot high and she spat up at me when she spoke. When I fell back away from her, she took her shoe off and hit me on the leg. Her eyes never stopped moving.

'Why are you looking at me?' she asked, as she hit me. I hadn't even started to do the combination when she smacked me and said, 'No, do it again.'

I decided to cry, because I wanted to get out of the class. It wasn't hard to make myself cry as I was always on the verge of tears in her class.

She walked away and when I stopped she came over and asked haughtily, 'Have you finished?'

I started sniffling again. I thought she was going to kick me out but she didn't. In fact, it just got worse. I don't think we did any ballet that day. She just stood there and pushed me around. The reason I kept crying was because I was in bits and I thought I was losing my mind. I cried for about 20 minutes until I had no more tears left. She didn't go near me for the rest of that day; she didn't really go near anyone, but we finished class early for a change.

I cried more often after that but when I was crying the other girls just stood there with their eyes down. There was no support from anyone. At this stage, only a week into the term, we were all beaten down.

I took the whiplash for three people in class. Because Anna was so gentle, she didn't give out to her; she didn't understand the Japanese girls or she was afraid of them— I'm not sure which. I was the only foreigner in her class that got smacked so badly. I used to have bruises on my arms and all the way down the back of my legs, but Sakharova hated people seeing them. If we came into class with a bruise she would insist that we came in the next day wearing a long sleeved leotard. She didn't want to see the bruises. I've seen her scrape through tights with a key until she drew blood. Her favourite mode of punishment with me was to hit me on the side of my head with her bunch of keys.

She would sometimes just give us a wallop as she was walking by. I didn't mind those slaps so much. Once she kept on walking it was fine.

She beat me everyday: with her hands, her shoes, her keys; she'd scrape my legs, and she'd pull my hair. It was almost like she was trying to break my spirit.

It started to affect Anna and I more and more. I used to wake up crying when Donna would leave to go to class because I didn't know what to do. We used to go down to the bathroom and have a cigarette before class because we were so scared. We had to smoke because we were a bundle of nerves. We would sit on the window ledge of the second floor looking down.

Most of the time we wouldn't even have to talk. We just sat in miserable silence, psyching ourselves up for the class ahead.

Whenever I wore short sleeves, everyone could see my bruises. I tried telling Donna and she would be sympathetic for a couple of minutes. I think it probably was hard for people to believe how badly we were treated.

No one had really spoken about her class and none of the girls ever revealed how bad she was.

The rest of the day was completely wasted. Myself and Anna came back so wrecked we were often allowed to skip Russian. I had decided I would stick the class for as long as possible, but I knew that I would end up hating ballet if I stayed in this environment. It was likely that I would go home for Christmas and not bother coming back.

Anna and I were in a terrible state. We weren't eating properly and I was smoking very heavily. Things were really bad. I used to have diarrhoea every morning and night. I used to shake and cry. I felt as if I was having a nervous breakdown and I was severely depressed. Anna wasn't much better.

I was treated worse than anyone else in the class. She tried to let people know that she was going to invest a lot of time in me but I knew this was not the way I needed to be treated. I was ready to give up by this stage. I couldn't handle it.

About two weeks after term began, she kneed me on the bum quite severely and bruised the area around my tailbone. I couldn't tolerate it any longer. When we finished class that day I was shaking. I stood at the barre and told Anna I wasn't coming back to the class. I felt physically sick. Anna came over, took my hand and looked at me with her big eyes and said, 'Yeah, let's never come back in here again.'

It was that simple. She was so nice.

'Come on, you'll be grand, you'll be grand.'

She started crying and I joined in, because the sheer thought of not returning to the class was such a relief. The Russians had no sympathy for us at all. They had been getting beaten for years, so they probably couldn't understand why we were so upset.

We went back to the Internat and sat on the window ledge in the toilet talking about how we were going to leave her class. We didn't talk to anyone else about it because we felt it was just the two of us going through the same thing at the same time. Even though Anna wasn't getting hit as much, there's nothing worse than seeing a friend upset. We were both in the same boat. We said we weren't going back, no matter what.

'I can't go back in,' I said to Anna. 'I've been on the toilet for two weeks and I'm depressed. Basically, I couldn't care less about ballet any more. I'm going home.'

The next day we didn't go into class. We hid in the toilets in the Internat giggling with nerves. We felt hysterical. We didn't go into the school that day at all and we never told any of the Irish students what we were doing. Sakharova didn't come looking for us, despite our fears. She must have thought we'd be back in class the next day, but the following morning we went straight into Pidemskaya.

Our Russian wasn't great but mine was slightly better than Anna's, so she nominated me to do the talking. I was very nervous about telling Pidemskaya we were leaving Sakharova's class, but Anna gave me strength.

'We're not going back into Madame Sakharova's class because she hits us,' I told Pidemskaya in one breath, before I could change my mind.

'Oh no, everything will be okay,' Pidemskaya said, looking puzzled. 'I'll get Madame Sakharova and see what this is about.'

She brought us into the corridor and knocked on Sakharova's office. Sakharova came out and asked us why were weren't dressed for class. I took several breaths before speaking. I was trembling with fear.

'We're not going back into your class.'

She looked at me and her jaw dropped. None of the Irish students had ever voiced concern about Sakharova's method of teaching. I braced myself for the onslaught.

'Why, what's wrong?' she barked.

I turned bright red and I hesitated, but I knew I had to follow this through. I simply couldn't go back into her class.

'Because you're hitting us.'

Anna grabbed my hand and I swallowed the lump that had started to rise in my throat and continued. 'No, we're not happy.'

'No, that's foolish and stupid. I'm a brilliant teacher. I am well known in Russia and all over the world.' Her nostrils flared and she bristled with indignation. 'How dare you tell me that you don't want to go to my class?'

'We're not going back into your class!' I said, standing my ground.

She narrowed her eyes, paused for a moment and then said, 'Well, you think about it. You come back into my class tomorrow. Yes? . . . Yes?'

'Okay,' I answered, not knowing what else to say.

I knew that if she stopped hitting me, she was going to ignore me for a year and I would get nothing out of her class. I asked Pidemskaya if we could be put into another class. She told us to go off and think about what we wanted.

Anna and I ran back to the toilets in the Internat and lit our cigarettes with shaking hands. We shook, laughed and cried for about an hour after that because we didn't know what was going to happen. Sakharova thought we were silly children that could be dragged back to class, but she didn't know how determined we were. I was prepared to go back to Ireland, rather than return to her class.

For the next two days, we didn't go near the school. We stayed in bed and didn't go to any class. We were afraid of bumping into Sakharova in the corridors. I was so depressed that I stayed in bed and was afraid to get up. On the third day, she came over from the school into my room. Donna had already left for her ballet class.

Sakharova stood in the doorway and said in a loud voice,

'Get out of bed and come to class.'

I had become more determined than ever in the time I had spent away. I didn't care what the consequences were by now. I would have preferred to go home than return to her class.

'No! If you don't give me another class instead, I'm going home and so is Anna.' Anna was dressed and she slipped into my bedroom and sat at the end of the bed. She told Sakharova we weren't going in. When Sakharova saw we hadn't changed our minds, she left.

We thought we were doing this quietly, on a one to one basis. We didn't want to cause a fuss and we still hadn't told any of our Irish friends what had happened. Little did we know that we had caused a big scandal in the school.

We later found out that Sakharova had gone into Svetlana's class looking for us. She gave out to them because we weren't in class but they hadn't a clue what was going on. Then word of what had happened spread. Dasha told me later that Sakharova came home very worried. She was so upset about us. We got to her in a way that no one else did.

Things escalated beyond our control as the ballet world in Russia is so tight-knit. There were many children in the school whose parents were working in the Bolshoi Theatre and Sakharova was worried about her reputation being damaged. The whole school knew we had left and there was an uproar about it.

Anna and I had missed two days of classes already, so we thought we'd better start attending the other classes at this point. After Sakharova left my room, we went over to Russian class. As we walked down the corridor to the classroom, we met Sakharova and hurried past her, but she came behind us, screaming and pushing us in front of the other students in the corridor. She had kept her cool until now, but I think when she saw that we weren't for turning, she lost her temper.

We arrived at the classroom crying and holding onto each other because we were so scared of this woman. When Russian class finished, Anna and I sat on the radiators at the window, staring into space. Sakharova came into the classroom after us. She beckoned at us to follow her out of the room. 'Come on!'

'No, we're not going. We're never going back into your class. If we don't get into another class, we are going home,' I asserted, and I sat back down.

Sometimes when you're a teenager, you are scared of people in authority but you still find the courage to stand up to them. I knew I would be wasting my parents' money and I would be wasting my time if I didn't change classes. The school got scared that we'd go home and it would be a big scandal, but I never thought it would get that far. I knew they'd put us into a different class; it was just a question of how long it took and how far it went. It was a very difficult and lonely time. I remember sitting on my bed crying and crying. The pressure on us was immense. Word got back to John Baraldi about what had happened and he rang us up. I took his call.

'Hi Monica. Is everything okay with you and Anna? What's happened with Sakharova?'

'John, this is the story,' I began. 'She beat both of us and we are both very sad. We can't eat; we can't sleep and I'm sitting on the toilet for 40 minutes every morning. We're crying all day. I'm not going back to that.'

I was getting upset just telling him about it and he could hear it in my voice.

'Okay! Okay, I'll sort it out. Don't worry. Everything will be fine.'

My mother was the next person to call. John had phoned her and told her what had happened.

'What are you doing, Monica? You're throwing away a big opportunity. What's happening?'

'Mam, if I went back into that class, I wouldn't come home the same person and not only that, I would end up hating ballet and I would give it up. I would be home at Christmas not knowing what to do with myself.'

I can understand that they were worried because all the Irish girls who had been in Sakharova's class previously had stuck with it, but myself and Anna couldn't. It's hard for me to say whether she treated us worse than the other Irish girls, because we weren't in their class. Either way, I just knew it was the wrong teaching method for me. None of the other Irish girls who had been in her class continued with classical ballet for long after they graduated.

We weren't particularly weak people, but I think Sakharova got worse as the years passed by. She expected so much from her students. Sakharova believed that beating us would enhance our performance. I think she wanted two foreign students to do exceptionally well in order to attract more foreign students to the school.

The foreigners were the only fee-paying students in the school. The Russian government paid for their own students. It didn't work out as she planned, however, because no more Irish students came to Perm once we all graduated that year.

Andre Joukov and I rehearse before our first show of *Giselle* in the Point Theatre, Dublin, 2003. © *The Irish Examiner*

Above: My bedroom in the Internat, Perm, 1992.

Below: Standing in front of the Perm State Theatre are, (from left): Nicola McCarthy; our Russian teacher, Eleana; Claire Rooney, me, Donna Addie, Caitríona Lowry, Catherine Loane, James Dunne, Katherine O'Malley, Anna Moore, Claire Keating, Niclola Jane Mullan, Emma O'Kane and Ella Clark.

Above left: Donna and I rehearse in the corridor of the school.

Above right: Liuba, my first room-mate in the company, and I get ready to go on stage for *Serenade*.

Below: The family get together to celebrate Mam's birthday. (From left) Siobhán, me, Mam, Dad, and Eileen.

Perm State Theatre's corp de ballet in *The Sleeping Beauty*. Those wigs can be so painful!
(From left) Svetlana, me, Irina, Elena, and Marianna.

Above & below: *Ballet Spectacular 2004.* Alan Foley as Prince Siegfried, and me as Odette in *Swan Lake.* © *Kieran Tobin, courtesy of Cork City Ballet.*

Above: Gavin de Paor and I rehearse pas de deux in school.

Left: Dancing the pas de trois from *Swan Lake* on stage in Perm.

Right: Ilya Chithov and I perform *Melody* as part of *Ballet Spectacular* in Cork. I wobbled hysterically at the beginning, while trying to learn this difficult pas de deux. © *Johan Lemmers; Courtesy of Cork City Ballet*

Right: Posing with Lena Levina, Valintina Bykova and Elena Filatova after performing *Pere Gunt.*

Above left: Behind the scenes at the opening night of *Giselle. Courtesy of Vera Mcgrath.*

Above right: I immersed myself in Russian culture. I started to dress like my Russian friends before long.

Above: Ilya and I dance the Adagio from the second act of *Giselle* in the Nation Concert Hall, 2004. © *Photocall Ireland*

Chapter Eleven

After what seemed like an eternity, though it was only a few days, we got a phone call from John Baraldi saying he'd sorted everything out. He said we'd be going into Nina Petrova Costrova's class, starting the next day. He also told me that I would have to do another year in the school, because at 16, I was too young to graduate. He said I might be in Sakharova's class next year and asked if I was okay with that. I was just so happy to be out of her class for the moment that I didn't care. I would deal with next year when it came.

Costrova was a spinster in her 60s, who always looked very cross because she had pinched features, but she was actually very nice. She was tiny, bone thin, and was slightly hunched when she walked. She had long grey/black hair with two white stripes in it and never stood still.

Anna and I were over the moon to be there. We did pretty well in class. I got onto the back barre again and because it was a small class, we got to do more things. That year I became a stronger, more capable dancer. I was beginning to become more familiar with my body and the movements happened without a second thought. I enjoyed dancing for its emotional and expressive qualities, rather than its technique.

After a month or so I had really relaxed into the school and almost forgot how upset I had been at the beginning of the year.

Duet continued to be one of my favourite classes, despite Maxim's absence. Vitaly Dubrovin was my teacher and he was good fun; his classes were enjoyable. I was partnered with a boy called Tolia that year. His identical twin, Roma, was also in my class. Tolia and I danced well together and we always had a great laugh. Tolia's best friend was the most talented boy in the class; his name was also Sasha. He had raw talent that oozed from him with every movement. He could jump in the air and do triple turns or even three and a half turns. He could jump his own height, which is tremendously hard to do. The audience just loved him. He was small and quirky looking, and was always laughing and joking.

He had been in Gillian's class the previous year, but I had never really noticed him before. Roma was also in Gillian's class and had dated her. He was heartbroken when she didn't return. They continued to correspond for many years afterwards.

One day in early December, Sasha was crossing over from the school to the Internat with his hands in his pockets, deep in thought. Here was the guy that was always laughing, with a sorrowful look on his face. That's when I saw another side to him. We started going out shortly after that.

Later in the year, Sasha was up in my room with Donna and I when there was a knock at the door. A boy from one of the younger classes asked Sasha to come out. After a few minutes I went out to see what was wrong, but Sasha was nowhere to be seen. I went down to the toilet because I thought he might be having a cigarette there.

He was in the toilet, on the floor crying. Through his tears he told me his dad had died. The school had sent a little child over to tell him and then left him there. He was in a bundle on the floor sobbing his heart out and I sat there just holding him. I didn't know what to do or say. He didn't know what was going on, or even what had happened to his father. He only found out later that his father had died from pneumonia.

The assistant director sent some other children over to look for him so he could ring home from the school. But he didn't go over; he was so annoyed. He was so angry with the way Pidemskaya treated him. It was one of the most disgusting and appalling things I had ever witnessed in the school. It was a dreadful way to break the news to him. He had no support at all.

He came up to me two hours later with a tiny bag and said, 'I'm going home. Tell Tolia I'm leaving.'

'Do you have enough money? Is there anything I can do?' I asked, not knowing what else I could say or do. I wasn't able to go to the train with him, because I had classes and we weren't even meant to be dating other students. The teachers would never have excused me from class.

'No, I'm fine. I'll be back next week.'

It seemed so pitiful and lonely, not even having a friend to bring him to the train station. Nobody else knew what had happened. When the rest of the class found out they were very sympathetic. They kept asking me how he was but I didn't know.

He came back about a week later and seemed completely different. He didn't trust the system any more. He was angry with everyone. The teachers had treated him very badly. He became self-destructive and started to drink a lot. He rarely smiled after his father's death.

He reminded me of myself in a way—he couldn't pretend to be nice to someone if he didn't like them. He didn't like the assistant director so he was barely civil to her. Sasha didn't have a lot of luck in the school after that. He was supposed to be dancing main roles during the year for school performances, but he always seemed to be robbed of them at the very last minute. He would learn his part to perfection, and then some taller guy would come along and take his place.

He was always within arms reach of his big break, and they would take it away from him. I think that beat him down. He knew he was talented; everybody knew he was great but he wasn't getting a fair chance. So he stopped believing in himself. Having a good relationship with the artistic/assistant director was essential in the ballet school and theatre if you wanted to get decent roles.

Sasha could do things no one else could, and I always tried to support him and make him believe in himself once again.

I truly believe the reason God put him on this earth was to dance and to entertain people. He was a superb dancer and I was completely in awe of his talent.

By the time the exams came around I was fairly relaxed. The graduation exams were always held a month before the other exams, to give the students time to find work in one of the ballet companies before they closed for the summer.

I felt I was more than ready for the exams. I had done a good year in ballet and duet, and I went into them thinking that I was going to be doing them yet again a year later. Our duet exam was first and Gavin agreed to be my partner for it as Tolia was too small for me. Gavin already had three partners, so he substantially increased his workload as a favour to me. We danced well together and got a 5 in the exam so we were elated.

In the months coming up to the ballet exam, we had rehearsed the same combinations in ballet over and over again. I actually overlearnt them. It meant that I started to forget some things and I made a few small mistakes in the exam.

I'm not the type of person who gets caught up in mistakes during a performance, so I got over it but it seemed to set my teacher off. I didn't know what she was like at exam time. She was so melodramatic that she sprawled on the piano and hid her face in her hands. I thought the woman was having a heart attack and it was so unsettling, because she seemed like a really strong lady, but when it came to the crunch she was rocking herself in the chair with nerves. It really threw me. I spent the whole exam looking at her thinking, 'Oh my God, I must be dreadful.'

The Russian girls were familiar with her behaviour and they just ignored her. There was a committee assembled to examine us. It comprised senior members of the Bolshoi Theatre, the artistic director of Perm Theatre, the artistic director from Tchelyabinsk, and some members of Tartarstan Theatre. The exam finished and I got a 4, but I wasn't that concerned. I knew I wasn't focused enough, and Nina had really put me off.

I remember coming back to the Internat and being a little bit disappointed because I was expecting a 5. But I was thinking, 'Monica, it serves you right.' In the back of my mind I knew I had another year to fix it and it was hardly the end of the world.

I was getting changed and moping around the Internat when I found out they pushed my marks up to a 5. I was marked up because Sakharova wanted me back in her class the next year.

I was in great form for my character exam and I thought I did amazingly well. I had gone to every class with Anna and we had a great time during character that year. At the end of the exam, I was standing at the barre; I suppose I was posing. Ulanova, the teacher I had the year before, came up and tapped me on the shoulder.

'You are not really much of a character dancer, are you?' she smiled.

I started laughing out loud because I had tried so hard and I thought I was great. She couldn't understand why I found that funny.

'Sure, stick to the ballet, you're a good ballet dancer, not a good character dancer,' she reassured me.

Everyone was excitedly preparing for the graduation show. It was the culmination of three years of hard work. During one of the rehearsals three days before the show, Sakharova decided she had enough of certain students. She lost her temper with Anna initially and told her that she wasn't taking part in the show, which was the *Waltz of the Flowers* from *The Nutcracker*. She then turned around to a number of other students and told them they also were no longer required.

When I turned up for my rehearsal, I was sure I would be told the same. To my surprise, Gavin, James and I were among those selected to perform in the graduation show. The show went ahead and we all performed to a warm reception. Sasha, however, was the star and he stole the show. He was spectacular. He performed a dance called *The Gopak*. He ran out from the wings, jumped over his own height and did the splits in the air. There was an audible gasp from the audience. He received a standing ovation and did eight encores. The atmosphere was electric and I was very proud of him. The night after the performance, the graduating students were brought into the school theatre to receive their certificates. As each student is called, all the children in the audience cheer for them. As I wasn't receiving my diploma that year, I stayed in the audience and joined in.

I did celebrate with the others afterwards, though. We had a great night. We booked a restaurant and ate until we could eat no more. I had grown to love Russian food and I wolfed down winter salad and chicken. Afterwards we went to a disco and danced 'till the early morning. It's tradition that no one goes to bed at the end of graduation night; we all just walked around the city, sat in the park and had a laugh together, reminiscing about the last three years.

Chapter Twelve

John Baraldi had come over to Perm for the graduation. He reminded me that I would be in Sakharova's class when I returned.

'You know you're going back into Madame Sakharova's class next year.'

'I'll be fine,' I said. 'Next year will be different and I don't think she will beat me.'

'She might,' he replied, tentatively.

'I don't think so. It'll be fine,' I assured him. Sakharova had made a point of smiling at me every time she saw me in the corridor, therefore I thought our relationship had improved.

John went to Moscow for a couple of weeks and was coming back to Perm to collect me and accompany me home. All the other Irish students had accepted positions with various ballet companies around Russia. Most theatres in Russia, however, close for the summer, so we were due to fly home to spend the summer with our families.

Unbeknownst to me, my duet teacher, Vitaly Dubrovin went to Sakharova and said he wanted me to join the theatre. As well as teaching duet in the school, Dubrovin worked in the theatre as an assistant to the artistic director. Sakharova said she wanted me back in her class next year. But he insisted.

'I think Monica has gotten all she can get out of the school and I think she should be in the company,' he told her.

Dubrovin asked me if I would like to join the company and I said that I would love to; but I thought it was a hypothetical question. I didn't realise that he would take it as a definite yes.

Meanwhile, I continued going to class with Emma everyday. Everyone else had already left, but Emma's job in Gorky (now called Nizhni Novgorod) didn't start until September.

I knew that some of the committee who had examined us at the graduation exam had expressed interest in me, but I thought I couldn't start working until I was 18. I would only turn 17 the following month, so it made sense to attend the school for another year.

About two weeks before I was due to return to Dublin, I received a phone call. It was Dubrovin.

'Where were you?' he asked, sounding slightly annoyed.

'I was in bed.'

'Why aren't you in class?'

'It doesn't start until half past ten. I was in class yesterday.'

'No, not in the school! In the company.'

'What?'

He went on to say I had missed my first day of work.

This is how I found out I had a job in the Perm State Theatre—I didn't even know that everything had gone ahead. I thought when he had asked me to join the company, he meant the following year. He obviously knew it was a great honour to be offered a job in the company and I would be delighted, so he wondered where I was.

I ran upstairs, got dressed, and started looking for Sasha.

He had just found out that I had joined the company as well, and he was on his way to tell me.

I was thrilled, but it then occurred to me: how was I going to tell my parents? They would probably worry about me becoming a professional ballet dancer at such a young age. I pushed the thought aside. I would deal with that later. For now I was just so happy.

Three days later, my former Russian teacher, Elena came down to me and explained what had happened. Elena told me that when Sakharova found out I'd been contracted to the theatre, she fired Dubrovin. So once again, there was war over me. After much arguing, though, Sakharova had agreed to let me join.

'Listen, I'm going to get your diploma for you now,' Elena said, 'before Madame Sakharova changes her mind. Go now while you still can.' She went over and got everything signed and sealed. Dubrovin and Elena arranged it quickly and quietly because they were afraid Sakharova was going to back out.

Elena came back to the Internat and gave me my diploma certificate. 'That's it. Now you are officially graduated.'

Once I realised I was now employed by the company, I headed into work the following morning. I hadn't a clue where to go though. I met Liuba, a girl from the fifth floor who had also joined the company, so I said I would go with her. As we reached the theatre, she remembered she hadn't locked her room. She showed me which door to enter and told me to get the lift upstairs while she ran back to lock her room.

On my way up, the lift ground to a noisy halt. I couldn't believe it. I kept my cool and pressed the bell. To my horror, it took three hours to get it moving again. Consequently, I missed another day of work.

When they finally got me out, Dubrovin was at the door, smiling at me.

'What is wrong with you?' he chuckled. 'You're having bad luck.'

'This is a really bad sign,' I said, laughing. 'I should go back to school.'

'I've been fired because of you, so get over here!' He gave me a quick tour around the theatre. On the third day I finally made it into class to discover everyone was pretty much established. I really felt like the new girl.

I was the first foreigner to have ever joined the company as well as the youngest, so I felt completely out of place. I hadn't a clue what I was doing. I didn't even know where to get changed. I went into the big changing room that Dubrovin had showed me. Most of the female dancers were in their 20s and 30s; they seemed really old to me. I had watched these people perform in the ballet for years and I thought they were just fabulous. I was so intimidated.

Some of the women had their children in work with them. You have to remember that I had never been in a Russian changing room. Until now I always changed with the Irish students. I had never been fully submerged in anything Russian so when I walked in, I felt uneasy. I said a formal 'hello' and sneaked into a corner. They were all very apprehensive and didn't know what to think of me. It was quiet for a few moments and then I sneezed.

After a moment's hesitation someone came over to me and said, 'God bless you.' I didn't know how to answer so I just said 'excuse me'. In Russia, you are supposed to say 'thank you', so they all just started to giggle. I turned bright red and went into the classroom. I took a position at the end of the side barre so no one would see me. The back barre was absolutely jammed with people. There was only about three inches between the dancers and there was no room to breathe .

I could tell everyone was checking me out because for one thing, I was foreign and for another, I was late. They knew I had overslept the first day and I had been stuck in the lift on the second, so this was a source of great amusement. We did ballet class and it only lasted an hour, which I loved because it was half an hour less than in school.

After class, we rehearsed for Swan Lake. All the new girls stood at the back trying to learn. Sasha had been in a separate ballet class and he joined us for rehearsal. He stood beside me at the barre.

The woman who took the rehearsal class was called Valintina Bykova. She came up to me. 'What's your name?'

Sasha spoke for me. 'Monica.'

'I didn't ask your name; I asked her name. What's her name?' she said, with a hint of annoyance.

'Monica,' I replied, wondering why she was singling me out.

'How old are you?'

When I told her I was 16 she lost her temper.

'This isn't a créche! 16?' she shouted. 'We've never taken in 16-year-olds before,' and with that she stormed out.

I thought I was going to get fired. I was standing there feeling lousy, with Sasha reassuring me. I was so embarrassed. Some of the Russian girls came over and started rubbing my arm. I later learned that this is a characteristic of the Russians; they always rub you if you're upset.

I was on the verge of tears when the teacher came back in and sighed to no one in particular. 'Well, once I don't have to change her nappy.'

'Can you even speak Russian?' she asked me directly.

'Yes, of course I can.'

'Good! Learn that part,' and she pointed at one of the girls in the corps de ballet.

So I started learning a part from *Swan Lake*, which meant I was standing beside the barre just copying the girl she had gestured at. Eight of us joined the theatre from the school that year, which is more than usual. I was put in right down the back. I think the teacher saw potential in me, but thought I wasn't good enough to do much at that moment, so I was stuck at the back all the time. I didn't care where I stood; I was thrilled just to be there.

I was only in one show before I went home that summer. The other new students got a part in almost everything because it was easier to teach them than it was to teach me.

I still had difficulty with the language. I could speak it and understand it most of the time, but I had to work harder to understand the instructions.

I had to come in for every performance, to watch and learn the ballet, and I enjoyed that because Sasha and some of my friends were performing in them. As a result, I found myself looking at ballet from a different point of view. It wasn't glamorous anymore; it was just hard work.

While I was in school, I looked at them in awe, but when I was backstage, I knew I would be dancing those ballets next and it was going to be really tough. I never went out into the audience; I always stood in the wings because I could familiarise myself with how people behaved on stage.

I learnt that some people talked, some people whispered, the people with a nervous disposition laughed—anything could happen. I remember one time I was dancing in *Swan Lake* and my lace came undone. I did my turn, stepped back into the wing, tied my lace, and came back out. Nobody even noticed. You get so familiar with the stage that you can do this. That's what I was looking for in the early months. I wasn't only trying to learn the steps; I was trying to see what you could do and what you could get away with.

Every day when we came in, we'd perform a different ballet. The company had 30 ballets in their repertoire so it was mind-boggling. I thought I would never be able to remember them all. I would have just started learning one ballet when the next day, we would be doing a different one altogether. I didn't even know where to stand or who to copy.

People were so protective of their places because they had worked so hard for them. They didn't particularly want to learn a new place in the corps. The only time they were willing to do this was when it was a bigger and better role. We didn't want to practise someone's part in case they thought we were stepping on their toes. We had to be told what part to learn every day.

There were some days I would come in and there would be a full rehearsal out of the blue. The Russians called this *praygon* and it's similar to a full dress rehearsal, but they don't put on their make-up.

My first show was *Swan Lake*, which the company performed only two weeks after I joined. I couldn't believe that after a fortnight, I was performing in the theatre as a professional ballet dancer. I was so excited.

Before the show I was told to get my outfit sorted out, so I went into the costume room. There were hundreds of costumes lined up on a wall and I hadn't a clue which one I was supposed to wear. I couldn't read the names that were written in Russian on the inside of the costumes.

I remember just walking around, because I was too shy to ask anyone for help.

'Where in God's name am I? What am I going to do?' I was thinking as I flicked through the rails.

I came out and walked down the corridor to where there were more rails with costumes. My teacher was passing by and I asked her what costume I was supposed to have. She nearly had a fit.

'Do I look like a costume lady to you? Do I? Well, I'm not. Ask them.'

I looked at her in frustration as she walked off. One of the principal dancers, Natasha Moiseeva, overheard the conversation and came up to me.

'I'll bring you to the costume lady,' she said genially and then she looked at me in amazement. I was wearing thick brown eye make-up and had big bushy eyebrows. I didn't have any false eyelashes on and I wasn't wearing any blusher. I was like any 16-year-old who was told to put on stage make-up without any guidance.

'You should be wearing blue eye make-up, you know. Come with me.'

She brought me into the dressing room, sat me in her chair and re-applied my make-up. Some of the girls had already given me colours that didn't suit them. I had a lot of make-up but I didn't know how to use it. Natasha gave me an impromtu lesson and finished by drawing some lines along my eyes.

'These make your eyes look wider, especially for stage. The lights are so bright they make your face look white, so everything is supposed to be really marked out, including your cheeks and eyes.'

Proper make-up application is part of the lore passed on in Russian generations, so by the time Russian girls get to my age, they are already proficient in its use.

I started to pick up tips about hair and make-up as I went along. It probably took me about five years to figure out what really suits me for the stage. I can now do my hair and make-up in about 15 minutes.

Natasha then asked one of the other girls to bring me up to the costume lady. No one had been allocated to help me acquaint myself with the theatre. I only found out the way things worked because some of the girls were so kind to me.

The costume lady gave me a white tutu and luckily enough, it fitted me and I was finally ready to go on stage.

I had never done *Swan Lake* before although I had done sections of it in school. We had never rehearsed the first act; all we ever did in school was the second act, which includes the famous *Cygnets* dance.

In my first performance with the company, I played a lady-in-waiting in the first act, which meant I simply had to walk on stage, bow twice, and walk off again. I nearly got weak doing that, however, because it was my very first time as a professional. I hadn't a clue when I was supposed to bow, so this was a big deal to me.

I also got to do the fourth act, which is 25 minutes of dance; it's not a particularly hard dance but when you don't know what you're doing, it's awful. The curtain came up and we started. I was told what to do from start to finish. The people in front of me and behind me talked me through every step. They tugged on my tutu when it looked like I was going off in the wrong direction. I must admit that I might as well have been a blind woman.

There were three new dancers on the stage and the girls whispered instructions to each of us throughout the performance.

I will always remember that particular performance because I lost my concentration mid-way through the show when I saw Sasha standing in the wings. He distracted me and I broke out into a cold sweat.

'Are you okay?' Sasha whispered.

I was glistening. Even my hair and legs were wet. I forgot what I was doing. I got a severe dose of stage fright and I just wanted to walk off.

Everything happened really quickly towards the end and there was a lot of changing lines. I just stood there and I couldn't move. Some of the older dancers realised what had happened and they literally dragged me from one position to another. I was lucky because

I was between two older women who were nearly retired, and thus very experienced. These two particular women were exceptionally nice and I was very lucky. I remember standing there at the end, still sweating. Sasha was embarrassed because his girlfriend had performed badly. All the Russians were really cool and I was like a lump of jelly. I remember him standing there in the wings, shaking his head. We did the bow and afterwards I couldn't move; I just stood on the stage in shock.

After every new dancer appeared on stage for the first time, they were congratulated and in return had to buy everyone a drink. It just hit me that I had now turned professional. I also realised it was time to tell my parents.

The next day, we finished for the summer. I met John Baraldi with the rest of the Irish students in Moscow and it was great to see everyone after a short break, but it felt like a lifetime.

We flew back to Dublin and I was delighted to see my family once again. The following day I went for a walk with Dad and the dog, and I decided the time was right to break the news.

'Dad, I'm after joining a company,' I began.

'What? But you are too young.'

'Dad, it just happened. I'm sorry. At least I won't be spending your money on the tuition. They promised they would look after me.'

Dad asked me why I hadn't told him sooner.

'It just happened. It literally, honest to God, just happened! But although I didn't plan it, I think I've gotten as much as I can from the school.'

Although I didn't admit it to myself, let alone to Dad, I was actually quite nervous about turning professional. I hadn't a clue what I was letting myself in for, and because Dubrovin had been fired from the school because of me, I felt obliged to stay with the company.

'They'll take care of me in the company,' I assured him. 'And Sasha is there as well, if I need help with anything.'

After attending Perm school for three years, Mam and Dad now had confidence in the Russian system. They knew I had been well looked after, but more importantly I was focused on my ballet.

The fact that Sasha was in the company as well made Dad feel better, because it meant I wasn't all by myself. We discussed all the options. He pointed out the advantage of returning to the school. It certainly was the safer option, and I was tempted for a split second, but I knew I couldn't go back. I could only go forward, where ever that may bring me.

Chapter Thirteen

When I returned to Perm as a member of the ballet company, I was on my own. The whole support network I was used to had vanished. I was now 17-years-old and a professional ballet dancer. All my former classmates had moved on to other jobs and other cities.

John Baraldi didn't bring any more students to Perm. I'm not sure why he decided not to continue with the programme, but it ended that year anyway. I was lucky to receive the training I did.

I moved into the hostel that the theatre provided to some of its staff. In 1918 this building was a hotel. Prince Mikhail Romaivov took refuge there during the Russian Revolution. He was recognised and arrested, taken out, and shot. I could see that it had once been grand and beautiful, but now it was shoddy and dilapidated. Between the opera, the orchestra, and the ballet, the theatre employed close to 1000 people, and they rented a floor in this historical building. I shared a room with Liuba, while another dancer, Lena, was just down the hall.

We were the only ballet dancers who lived in the building. The other floor was rented by the Institute of Culture. The people living on that floor were all 18 or 19-year-old students, who were doing a managerial course in culture and the arts.

Our hostel was a 25-minute tram ride from the theatre and a motley crowd lived there. It was a dreadful place. There was only one working shower and one working toilet on the whole floor, which was shared by 50 people. The shower was just a cubical with a wooden door. There was no common-room.

The kitchen was filthy. It had two aluminium sinks and two cookers, which had gradually stopped working. We shared the kitchen with children, women, and men, who were constantly walking around in their shorts, vests, nightgowns, underwear, and flip-flops.

One of the women used to wash her baby's bum in the sink, while I often stood there preparing food. She'd whip off the terrycloth, put the waste into the sink, and wipe her baby down. Nobody would say anything to this woman; she was big and burly and would have no problem slapping you if you commented.

The bedroom Liuba and I shared was an average sized room. My bed was on one side and Liuba's was opposite.

During the winter the room froze. Ice would form on the inside window pane on particularly cold days. Although there were two panes of glass in the window, it was a far cry from the double glazing we had in Ireland. In the winter, if we wanted something frozen, we put it on the outside ledge; if we just wanted to keep the food cool, we left it on the inside ledge. The temperature drops to minus 30 degrees in the winter in Perm. We could gauge how cold it was outside by the level of frost on the window; sometimes we couldn't even see through the glass because it was covered in thick ice and frost.

There were no washing machines, but it was even worse than the Internat, because there was no drying room. The water was so cold that it would burn your hands. I often just soaked my clothes in a cold basin, because there was no hot water; this was a rare commodity. I eventually ended up throwing some of my clothes out because they became mouldy.

The lack of hot water made my life hard. I couldn't simply come home and have a shower; instead I used to shower in the theatre, because at least the showers always worked there. I would sometimes boil a kettle to wash my hair in a basin, but my day would be slowed down by two hours, just by the lack of hot water. I had to wash my hair everyday because it would be so caked with hairspray after a performance.

I was looking forward to going back to work and settling into the company. The Russian language remained my biggest obstacle. Even though I had lived in Russia for three years, I had never fully grasped the language because I had spent most of my time with Irish girls. When I went back for my first ballet class, I was in the big changing room with all of the girls when Bykova called me out.

The whole room jokingly howled 'Woah!' indicating that I was in trouble. She brought me into her changing room, where the principal dancers and teachers got changed.

Bykova had decided I was timid enough for her room, as she only wanted quiet people there. There were only five other people that used this changing room. Among them was a lady called Rimma Shlyamova, who taught all the principal dancers. She could lose her temper at the drop of a hat.

Rimma Siraeva, who was a principal dancer, also changed here. I had admired her from afar when I was a student in the school. She had been in the company for about 13 years and I was completely in awe of her.

It wasn't an ideal room for a beginner because I was too timid and shy to have a conversation with them. Most people wouldn't want to be there, anyway, because the atmosphere was too disciplined.

But life went on and I slowly began finding my feet in the theatre. I discovered that the teacher hung the rehearsal schedule in the hall on the ground floor and it was updated regularly. Everyone congregated around to see when the next rehearsal would take place. This was how they knew when to get ready for the dress rehearsals.

It took me about two weeks to realise this. I had been stumbling upon dress rehearsals until I learnt this small but vital piece of information. A few weeks after returning, I was with everyone crowding around the board trying to see when the next rehearsal would take place, when the artistic director of the company, Kyrill Shmorgoner, came over to me. I hadn't met him yet, but I knew who he was.

The first thing he said to me was, 'I hope you have a rich family and friends to bring us to Ireland,' in a half-joking/ half-serious manner.

I was astounded. I felt that he was sending a signal to my colleagues that the reason I had been asked to join the company was because I could bring them to Ireland. I didn't know how to respond, so I just ignored his comment and went back to looking at the board. I couldn't believe the artistic director would say something like that to me but I brushed it aside and just got on with things.

We opened the season with *Swan Lake* and I had the same part in Act Four, so I felt a lot more confident going on stage than the previous time, and I got through it without the same nerves. I was still unsure of the moves, but I listened carefully to my colleagues' whispered instructions.

The Sleeping Beauty was our next show and everyone had to wear a wig in this ballet. There was a lady in the theatre who was tasked with looking after the wigs and fitting them on us before the performance. They had hundreds of wigs in the theatre. All the white and coloured wigs, such as those used in *The Sleeping Beauty* and *The Nutcracker* were made out of horse hair. All the other hair pieces, such as the ones used in *Giselle* and *Swan Lake* were made from human hair. The wigs are notoriously expensive and it takes years to get your own wig in a company. It probably took me longer than most in Perm as they thought I wouldn't stay with the company for very long because I was Irish. The people who made the wigs in the company also made the eyelashes.

I dyed my hair black that year because there was only one other girl with black hair, and I thought it was so much more striking. I soon discovered there were two black hairpieces (Extensions that clip onto the hair) and only two of us with black hair, so we got them without question. The other girls ended up fighting over the blonde hairpieces.

When you are new to a company, however, there are no wigs allocated to you, so the wig lady must experiment and try to fit you into any wig that will remotely work. Whether it feels comfortable or not doesn't really matter.

Because my own hair was long, trying to find me a wig wasn't easy, so she just took one from the pile and pinned it to my head. I felt as if someone had placed a vice grips on me. I could hardly keep my head up.

When she left I just sat there and looked into the mirror. My eyes were watering and I could barely keep them open as there were so many pins in my head. In fact, when I looked closer, I could see my eyes were red with pain.

My head was throbbing and I hadn't even been on stage yet. There was an hour to go and I didn't know if I could hold out until the performance. I couldn't tell her it was sore because I was afraid that I'd seem arrogant.

I had scarcely said ten words to Rimma since I'd joined the company, but I was so stunned with the pain that I turned around to her and said, 'Is it supposed to be this bloody sore?'

Russian people rarely swear, especially in front of their elders, but Rimma just started laughing. She said she would be back in a minute and left me with my head resting on my hands. She returned a few minutes later with the wig lady and said, 'Take the wig off this girl. She's in obvious pain—get her something else.'

The wig lady fitted another one on me, and although it was still fairly painful, it was a huge improvement.

I was too embarrassed to say anything else because I didn't want to appear difficult. The wig lady went back to the other changing room and I thanked Rimma for her help. She started to giggle.

'I just felt so sorry for you; they weren't supposed to kill you.'

With that the ice was broken and we started to chat. At least now I was able to concentrate on dancing, and I really needed to concentrate. As everyone wore wigs on the stage, it was almost impossible to tell who was dancing around me, and I barely knew their names.

Most dancers remember what it's like starting out and luckily the majority of them were very nice to me. Once again from the start to the finish, they told me what I should be doing, and I got through another performance without any mishaps.

Not everyone in the company welcomed me, however. Because I wasn't fluent in the language, I didn't learn the roles as quickly as the Russian ballet dancers. There were so many ballets and so many roles that I was utterly overwhelmed at the beginning. Perm Theatre normally performs 13 ballets a month and it rarely repeats the same ballet twice in a month.

When I had enough time to learn a piece I was fine but if I was unsure of my part or if I felt under pressure,

I would be covered in a cold, nervous sweat midway through the performance.

I was terrified in rehearsal, because if Bykova said something to me and it didn't click straight away, I was in deep trouble.

After *The Sleeping Beauty* I was in a ballet called *La Sylphide*. I had a simple role in the second act and we performed this two nights in a row.

After the second performance, a woman in the company called Irina came up to me and said, 'I was in the audience last night and you were awful. You have short legs and short arms, and you're like an old woman. You have a hump in your back.'

Irina was one of these people who bullied new girls, and she had been aloof with me prior to this, but never directly unpleasant. I just stood there not knowing what to say, and she went to her friend Svetta and asked her if it was true.

Svetta agreed with her, and I later learned that Svetta would agree with her about anything. She never had anything to say on her own behalf. They said I was too short; I was looking down; I had a hump on my back; I wasn't pretty—the list was endless. It went on and on.

'If only you knew how hard I was trying,' I thought. Tears slowly streamed down my face. Liuba saw me crying and came over to tell them to leave me alone. 'The two of you might be better than her now, but just you wait.'

Liuba was great; she was so confident. She found everything easier than I did. She had long legs and fair hair that fell to her shoulders. Her face was a perfect oval and she had deep blue eyes. She was tremendously affable and was liked by everyone. She was doing much better than I was in rehearsals, and in the shows.

Despite Liuba's assistance, the two women continued to make life hard for me. They were so familiar with my teacher that they went to her and said how utterly out of place I looked.

As a result, Bykova paid particular attention to me, but it wasn't the type of attention I desired. For the next year she bullied me and tried to intimidate me into leaving the company.

She also picked on Veronika, who had given me a hard time in second year in school. She had joined the company when she graduated the previous year. Despite the bullying that Veronika had subjected me to, I took no pleasure in seeing her receive similar treatment.

If someone else did something wrong while dancing, Bykova would simply correct them, but if I did something wrong the music would stop and she would come over to me. She took pleasure in harassing me.

'What are you doing here; why don't you just go back to England?'

She thought England and Ireland were the same place.

'Why don't you go back to your England? We don't want you here; you are no good. I don't know why you are here; you don't get any money; you live in an awful place; why don't you go back to your England? Or are you a spy? You must be a spy.'

All the men and women would be rolling around laughing. She would continue in this manner.

'Ah no, you are not a spy. You have too much of an accent! I don't know what to make of you. You are not that bad. Why can't you get a job in your England?'

I wanted to say to her, 'You fucking, ignorant bitch! I'm not even from England,' but I was so anxious and nervy that words always failed me.

After a while I started to laugh along with her and I found that would deter her and she would walk away from me a little earlier.

I wasn't good at cooking and occasionally I found myself wishing I could go back to the old school canteen to eat, which I would have laughed at had someone said it to me a year previously.

One time I bought some red cabbage to make soup and when I boiled it, the mixture turned bright blue. The Russians in the kitchen were standing around looking at my pot with a mixture of horror and curiosity. They laughed at me and I got really annoyed because

I wanted to experiment without people interfering. I wanted to make my own mistakes in my own time. Everyone was on top of each other in the kitchen.

There was a canteen in the theatre and I'd sometimes eat there—but coming up to Christmas I got a bug and gastroenteritis after a visit to it. I was a grey pasty colour and I rapidly lost weight.

I felt so bad that I could barely get out of bed, but I dragged myself into the theatre, because I was afraid not to turn up for class. When I got into work, Rimma said I looked awful. I told her how dreadful I was feeling; I felt that I was going to be sick all of the time. She said she would sort it out with the teachers.

Rimma was best friends with Bykova because Bykova's husband died while she was on tour one time, and Rimma came back with her and supported her through it. They were almost like mother and daughter.

I was hunched against my dressing table when Bykova came in and tapped me on the back.

'What are you doing here? You are just taking up somebody's place. I have no time for people who are sickly. I have no time for it, don't you understand?'

I had no time for it either and I had little time for her bad disposition. I needed some help and a little sympathy wouldn't have gone astray. I didn't know where to go so Rimma brought me to the hospital, where they did an endoscopy. It was a horrible experience as they didn't give me any drugs to make me drowsy. I kept on gagging and retching on the tube.

The doctor said I had really bad gastric problems, so I brought in a note from him and she eased off on me then.

My gastric problems lasted about three months and I could only have porridge and rice everyday. They were the only things I could eat that didn't make me vomit. I was like a walking skeleton, which I didn't mind so much, but I didn't have any energy. I couldn't even eat any chocolate because it would burn my stomach.

I just drank about 20 cups of black tea a day, and I'd put lemon in it occasionally to break the monotony. Every now and then I would treat myself to a tomato.

Apart from my health, I started to develop problems with my feet and legs. Most ballerinas and dancers have problems with their joints and feet, and my problems were exacerbated because I wasn't able to rest them. My toes used to get sore and bruised and this really got me down.

It was like having a constant joint injury because my body didn't get a chance to recover. One day the nail on my little toe fell off. It looked disgusting, but I wasn't completely horrified. I knew it was likely to happen sooner or later. I had seen the deformities the other professional dancers had. My other toenails soon followed suit. My little toenails are so weak now they just peel off like the paper shell that surrounds an onion.

My big toenails sometimes lift right off the toe, except for a small area at the base, which is still attached to the skin. In order to dance I have to create a barrier between the nail and the toe, so it won't irritate the skin. My foot gets swollen like a ball but I've learned to live with the throbbing pain; although I never fully got used to it. By the end of the first year in the theatre, layers of skin would come off the back of my feet. Parts of my heel would wear down to the flesh underneath, and I would put layers of plaster over them. It was unbearable walking, never mind dancing.

At times I thought I was going to pass out with the pressure on my feet because there was raw flesh rubbing against my ballet shoes. If I didn't bind them enough, the blood would come through my pointe shoes.

I have since learned a few tricks to look after my feet. I fasten my toes tight with plaster, but there are still sometimes red sores on my feet. I often cut holes in my ballet shoes to alleviate the pressure. I'm quite blessed, really. Compared to some dancers, my feet aren't that bad.

By the time my parents came over in April, life had gotten a little easier. I was in most shows, but I was nowhere near the front by any means.

My parents met all of my friends and they saw where I lived. I think my mother was horrified, but Dad thought a little hardship was character building. They brought me two suitcases full of food, which I was so thankful for. I was using aluminium delft as it meant I could put my cup directly onto the stove and heat my tea without hanging around waiting for the kettle to boil. This particular habit of mine made my mother wince and she said I looked like someone in a concentration camp. It was like a holiday having them around. They brought me books, videos, shampoos, and luxuries such as chocolate bars, hot chocolate, and pop tarts.

They didn't like the fact that my room was so close to the kitchen, but it had its good points as well as its bad points. It was great to be able to run in and grab something quickly, but everyone used to congregate there and we'd hear laughter and noise in the middle of the night.

There were even wedding receptions held in our building and people would often get drunk and run up and down the corridor, and knock on our door. One time I caught two people having sex on the floor outside the toilet. I recognised the girl from the theatre, and he was someone else's husband.

I went over, kicked them and shouted at them to get up and leave. They were both drunk and barely noticed, so I got a basin of freezing cold water and threw it on top of them. I was trying to get some rest before a performance.

As they scrambled for their clothes, I screamed at them to leave the floor, but they hurled abuse at me. I called them every name under the sun because they didn't live in our building; he lived in an apartment block beside the theatre and I thought he shouldn't be dragging his business to my door. He looked as if he was going to give me a couple of slaps at one stage, but I was so outraged I just bullied them off the floor and then I locked the door with a bolt. I didn't need that going on under my nose and I didn't want any of us to get a bad reputation for what went on in this place.

A lot of girls who lived in the building claimed to be ballet dancers, when in fact they only started dancing at 18 or 19, and they didn't dance in the company at all. They gave the real ballet dancers a bad name, and people thought it was either Liuba, Lena or myself that were acting in this manner. We were very tame compared to the rest of them.

Chapter Fourteen

I got into a routine sooner than I expected. The theatre staged a ballet every Wednesday, Friday, and Sunday, and an opera every Tuesday, Thursday, and Saturday. It closed on a Monday, so that was my day off.

I got up at eight o'clock everyday, had breakfast, went to class, had a three-hour rehearsal and then some lunch. On the days of the performances, I would generally go to bed for a couple of hours between rehearsal and the show. I'd then get up, have a cup of tea and a bar of chocolate before I'd go into work to be on stage for seven o'clock.

When we had a performance, we didn't finish until 11 o'clock, and the trams stopped running at midnight. We had to be showered, dressed, and out as quickly as possible. It was never just as simple as getting dressed and going home. We would have to queue for the shower, either in the theatre or the hostel. I would then have something to eat because I'd be starving after dancing all night. By the time I'd get home, have some food, and wind down with a cup of tea, it could be one o'clock in the morning. I had to start again at eight o'clock the following morning. Eight years later, my routine is pretty much the same.

When I first joined the company, I was told that all of the new girls were contracted at the same rate of pay and at the same level. Prima ballerina's are on 18, which is the highest rate of pay; principal dancers are on 17; soloists and principal dancers are on 16; corps de ballet dancers who do the occasional solo are on 15; and the corps de ballet are on 14.

But I got signed on at 12, which was for people who weren't fully experienced. I didn't discover this until after Christmas. Liuba and I were talking about how badly we were paid, when I realised I was getting less than her, so I went up to Dubrovin and asked him what was going on.

I was annoyed, not so much because of the money, although that was a factor of course, but because it was disrespectful to me. I was dancing a lot; almost the same amount as Liuba and Lena, and I was dancing considerably more than some of the other new girls.

He checked the books and said, 'Oh my God, you're right. I'll put you on 14 with the other girls.'

So he did, but they didn't back pay me. Two years later they put me on 15 and three years after that I moved up to 16 and a half. They were probably just taking a chance that I wouldn't notice, because I was the first foreigner in the company.

All of the people who joined the same year as me were hired on contract. The theatre traditionally took people in as permanent staff, but they discovered they couldn't fire people when they become too old to dance, so they started hiring dancers on contract in the last few years.

I suppose it's fair to say that perhaps Lena and I were tame compared to the other girls in our hostel. Liuba made her own contribution to giving ballet dancers a bad name. She was so easy-going that she would invite people into our room without a second thought.

Her choice of guest often left a lot to be desired. She would invite guys into the room after the show and they were just horrible. They were only interested in trying to get her into bed. I was often sitting on my bed at four o'clock in the morning waiting for them to leave.

These were older men, and I felt I couldn't just tell them to leave. After all, they were Liuba's guests, and they simply wouldn't have listened to me. They would bring bottles of beer, champagne, and vodka with them, and our room would turn into an impromptu bar.

I am a bad sleeper anyway, so I would be tired the following morning when it was time to go to class. Liuba never had a problem getting up, no matter what time she fell asleep. I soon discovered she had relationships with about two or three husbands from the company. By the end of that spring I couldn't stand living with her any longer because when one of these husbands would go missing, people would come to me and ask if I had seen him, and he would usually still be in my bedroom. I didn't want any part in this.

As the year drew on, I got to know when to make myself scarce. I would leave the room when the men would arrive. I had a lot of friends on the floor that were in the opera and orchestra, and I would tell Liuba I was going to be gone for an hour.

Giving her some privacy wasn't a problem in itself; it was the fact that the guys wouldn't go home. They would be so infatuated with her that some of them would even sit on stools in the corridor while we were asleep.

There were times when they have slept on the window ledge in the kitchen, just to be near her rather than going home to their wives.

A gradual tension built up between us because I felt she was abusing our friendship and I got tired of lying for her.

She was a better dancer than me, which meant she was given more leeway in the company. But I couldn't afford not to be nice to people because my relationship with Bykova was so bad. I needed people to be on my side.

Initially I was glad that I shared with Liuba, because I really liked her, but towards the end of the year, I couldn't take much more of these late nights. I went to Dubrovin and asked him to move me into a different room. I didn't say what Liuba was doing, because everyone knew what she was up to. I just said I needed another room. I had lost a lot of weight and I was drawn and felt washed out.

'This can't go on,' I said. 'Look at me! I'm not sleeping; I'm not enjoying work anymore. I haven't been able to sit down and relax for days.'

He said he wasn't able to do anything for me in the middle of the year, but he would place me with someone else the following year. But things happened of their own accord before Dubrovin had a chance to do anything. Liuba ended up having a drawn-out affair with yet another married man from the theatre. His wife was best friends with our prima ballerina, Elena Kulagina. Elena had more than enough reason to want Liuba out. Liuba was also having an affair with Elena's boyfriend at the same time.

So in the end, I didn't have to do anything. It was sorted for me. The prima went up to Kyrill, the artistic director, and gave him an ultimatum. She said it was either her or Liuba. One of them had to go.

There were too many bad feelings towards Liuba in the theatre by now. The artistic director asked her to leave and she was gone before the year was out.

I went home for the summer and had a great time. I completely relaxed and wound down. Donna was also home on holidays from Tchelyabinsk, and we enjoyed the holiday together. All too soon the summer was over, and when I returned to the company and the hostel in September, Dubrovin tried to talk me into sharing a room with someone new, but I literally blocked the door and said, 'No; not this year.'

I didn't particularly want to live in the hostel again, but I didn't have enough knowledge of the language to go out and rent an apartment on my own.

I felt that if someone found out there was a foreigner alone in an apartment, you wouldn't know what could happen because there were still few foreigners in Perm.

I had now learned to dress like a Russian girl, so no one knew I was foreign by simply looking at me. With my black hair and pale complexion, I could easily pass for an Eastern European. When I went shopping I would sometimes be afraid to ask for items, because there would invariably be a big queue of people behind me. I often ended up whispering what I needed and the assistants would shout at me to speak up.

Obviously I had a foreign accent, so people would be straining their necks to see what I was getting. They would sometimes follow me around out of sheer curiosity. It was quite scary because this often happened in the evening time when it was dark.

It got so bad at one stage that I wouldn't go out shopping at all. I was lucky I had Sasha to look after me, so I didn't feel completely alone. He did all of the shopping for me.

I was just so sick and tired of people shouting and staring at me.

Sasha was living closer to the theatre with the boys. Back then I thought my living accommodation was fine, but with hindsight I think I got a really raw deal. They should have changed things around and put the boys where we were, and the girls should have been closer to the theatre, for security reasons.

There were other places available that would have been more suitable for me, but the directors of the theatre never went out of their way to say, 'Look, she's a foreigner. We'll put her in an apartment.'

I was treated like the others when it suited them, but if anything went wrong, I was the foreigner. If I messed up in a performance, they would say, 'She's Irish.'

But if everything went right, they would never mention my country. They let everyone assume I was Russian.

Throughout my second year in the company, Bykova gradually stopped picking on me. I think she saw that I danced whatever role she wanted without complaining, and I tried so hard to do each role perfectly. She probably respected the fact that I listened to her criticisms and accusations of spying, smiled at her and then came back for more. When I returned to the company for another year, and she saw that I had no intentions of leaving, she started to respect me.

Bykova knew I wasn't doing it for the money—I could have gone to London or elsewhere and earned more. It was apparent that I was with the Perm State Ballet because I wanted to be there.

There was no sudden moment when she softened towards me, but the ice had slowly melted and it made my job so much more enjoyable.

My first tour with the company was to Austria at the end of my second season, and is memorable for all the wrong reasons. I was so excited and even the fact that it took three trains and one new undercarriage to get there didn't dampen my enthusiasm. We got the 'Kama' to Moscow and transferred there to another train that was to take us directly to Austria.

Unfortunately that train broke down somewhere in Poland, so we switched trains once more. When we reached the European border, they had to change the undercarriage to suit the European tracks. We were raised about six feet into the air while they did this and we couldn't stop laughing.

We went through Belarus, Poland, and Slovakia, stopping at each border to get our passports stamped.

When we got to the Belarus border, the guard checking the passports stole the register slip from my passport and refused me entry so I had to give him a backhander of $20 to get through.

The train journey to Austria took three and a half days, so by the end of it we were filthy and restless. The first town that we performed in was called Bruck; it was absolutely gorgeous. We danced *Don Quixote* that evening to a good reception, although the audience was quite small. But that sometimes happens at the beginning of a tour, so we weren't too concerned. The audience grows as people hear about it. News of the ballet is spread by word of mouth as well as the marketing drive but we noticed there weren't many big posters around the town.

We spent two nights in Bruck in a lovely hotel. It had a breakfast buffet where we could eat as much as we wanted.

We were so enthralled at seeing all this food that we ate everything we could. The next morning they changed breakfast from a buffet to a set meal to avoid a repetition.

We then moved to a place called Innsbruck in the Alps; the location for the Winter Olympics of 1964 and 1976. When we got to Innsbruck, it became very clear that the impresario for this tour hadn't spent any money on promoting the ballet. Nobody knew we were coming; it hadn't been advertised at all. This frightened the artistic director, Kyrill, who was accompanying us on the tour.

The first couple of nights were strange because there were so few people watching us. On our fourth night we performed in front of 20 people in a theatre that seated around 600. It began to worry us, as the company had never performed to empty theatres before.

The impresario usually waits backstage to greet us at the end of the show, and to make sure we get back to the hotel safely. At the end of this particular night, when we were packing up and getting on the bus, the impresario was nowhere to be seen. We went back to the hotel, not sure what was going on.

He had given us $10 each the previous night, so we all went out to dinner to celebrate Elena's birthday. We thought the impresario would be back the following day.

The next morning, however, Kyrill told us we were going home. He said the impresario had run out on us and we were broke. We didn't even have enough money to get back to Russia, and we didn't have return tickets for the train; we were left in Austria with nothing.

Kyrill was as shocked as we were. We just stood outside the hotel scratching our heads. I kept thinking, 'We've just been dumped in Austria.' I simply couldn't believe it. It was my first experience of touring with the company and I had always imagined it to be a glamorous experience. I certainly didn't expect to come across this type of situation.

We had a return ticket for the bus, so we left Innsbruck and travelled about 150 miles to the train station. We stopped off at a truck stop and I was absolutely starving. I had spent all of my money at dinner the previous night, so I didn't have a penny on me.

They sold freshly baked bread at the truck stop and it smelt divine. I was looking at a bun and I thought about stealing it, because I was so hungry, but I couldn't do it. Most of us hadn't any money, but some of the troupe had about three dollars left and they were able to buy a piece of bread.

I got back onto the bus angry, frustrated, hungry, and tired. There was plenty of wine on board, however, so it was being passed around freely. I wasn't really a drinker but I was so upset that I actually got quite drunk and fell asleep. When I woke up we were outside the train station.

We didn't know what was going on, but we didn't have any tickets, so we bombarded the ticket agent and explained that we had been dumped in Austria. When he showed no sign of understanding, we jumped on the train. We stood in the corridor waiting to see what Kyrill would tell us to do.

We breathed a collective sigh of relief when the train took off, but it hadn't even left the platform when it suddenly stopped. The inspector came on board and told us to get off. There was utter chaos. Nobody knew what was going on or what to do.

Then a woman from the Perm Institute for Culture and Arts called Lidiya, who was touring with us, bought us tickets with her own money. While she was paying for the tickets, we all took a cabin with bunk beds, because we assumed we would have sleeping cabins for the three day journey home.

Then Lidiya came back and broke the bad news to us; she didn't have enough money to buy those seats. She had only bought seated tickets and about nine or ten of us had to squash into a cabin like sardines.

Some of the lads had brought vodka with them, and they took it out of the bags before stacking the luggage in the corridor.

Everyone was starving, but in great spirits for some reason. We had a fantastic time singing and joking about our great trip to Austria. I was so young and carefree that the whole misadventure didn't bother me. I just looked upon it as a crazy experience that I would look back on and laugh at some day. I joined in the vodka drinking and singing and made the most of it.

The drama didn't end there. When we arrived at the Polish border we had to disembark and move to the front of the train. Some people lost belongings in the commotion, and one unfortunate boy named Alexandr, lost his passport and got kicked off the train.

The artistic director gave him a few dollars and told him we'd be back in Perm in two days and he would sort everything out. In the meantime, Alexandr was taken into custody by the Polish authorities because he didn't have a passport to prove who he was. There was nothing anyone could do for him. We watched in horror as he was taken away by the police; he wasn't even allowed to take any of his belongings with him. It was dreadful.

The following day we arrived in Belarus and when we got there, we thew a party because everyone had rubles, and we could buy lots of food with very little money. We knew we were almost home. Because we were closer to Russia, Lidiya could get money wired to her, so we got a proper cabin with bunks between Belarus and Moscow, which was an overnight journey.

When we finally arrived in Moscow, we were exhausted, but we were still in great spirits. We were so young that nothing really perturbed us. We were able to live without the luxuries, and sometimes without the essentials. We laughed all the way through the experience because there was nothing else we could do. We had a great journey from Moscow to Perm. It just seemed to be one big party the whole way back.

I never found out what happened to the Austrian impresario, but I do know that Perm lost a lot of money on shipping us there and back.

Alexandr returned three days after us, none the worse for his experience. He just laughed as he told us about his time as a 'guest' of the Polish government.

Soon after we returned from Austria, I made up my mind to leave Sasha because we hadn't been getting on too well.

He was very unhappy in the company and he was drinking heavily. I was starting to progress in the theatre at last and we barely saw each other due to our schedules.

We had gradually drifted apart over a long time, but it came to a head shortly after I returned from the Austrian tour.

The girl who lived next door to me in the hostel was called Elena Nazorva, and she was married to a football player called Jena.

Elena and I had gone out shopping together one day, when Sasha came to visit me. Jena saw Sasha knocking on my door and invited him to a bar for a few drinks. It was a national holiday, and that generally means everyone gets drunk in Russia. I guess it's similar to Ireland in that manner.

In their drunken stupor, they decided to visit some friends who lived a twelve-hour train journey away from Perm. They drank solidly for the next three days. Elena had hidden her money in the freezer, but Jena had taken all of it. She was understandably very upset, but because she was pregnant I tried to keep her calm. She was in a terrible state though, and when Jena rang her in a drunken state he didn't help matters. He was very abrupt and didn't seem to understand her concern.

She cried non-stop while he was gone and I was left to pick up the pieces. To make matters worse, Elena ended up having a miscarriage while they were gone, and I wasn't able to give her the emotional support she needed. By the time they came back I had taken Elena to the hospital. Her husband couldn't get over the fact that he wasn't with her during this time. Sasha walked in to my room upon his return and asked how I was keeping, in a completely offhand manner.

'You and me—it's finished,' I told him.

He didn't look too worried because Russian women never dump their men. 'Yeah right,' he replied.

'I am serious,' I emphasised. 'I'm not having any of this shit anymore. We can be friends but we're not together.'

I was so upset at Elena's trauma and Sasha could have shown a little more understanding and sympathy. He didn't believe that I was really finishing with him, so he came in to my room anyway, got something to drink and then left.

He came up the next day and knocked on the door. I opened it but I told him he wasn't coming in. It was finished. He asked me if he could come in just to talk, but I said it was definitely over, so there was no point. I closed the door and hoped he would get the message, but this started happening every day. Then he began coming up drunk and knocking on the door. He kept trying to get in to talk to me; but I continuously told him we had nothing to talk about.

I did see him around the company but not that often because we had different rehearsals. We were never in each other's pockets even when we were going out. When he eventually realised I was serious, all of the lads came up to my room and asked me why it was finished. I told them to leave me alone and mind their own business.

They were the ones that took Sasha out drinking all the time, so they could have him.

I ended up falling out with all the male dancers in the company for about two months. They called me the ice maiden, because I wouldn't have him back but I couldn't have cared less what they thought.

When Sasha realised we were truly over, he decided to move to Moscow. He had wanted to leave Perm for some time, but he wouldn't go without me. When we broke up, he decided to do what made him happy and I was thrilled for him.

I still remember the day he packed his bags. He came over, gave me a hug, and told me he was sorry. I told him I was still his friend. I remember looking out of the window at him. He had a little rucksack on his back and I was thinking as I watched him go, 'I hope you do well.'

I still loved him as a person though I never really loved him as a boyfriend. I think I got admiration confused with love. I'm delighted to say that he's done really well for himself and he's now dancing in America.

We have managed to remain on friendly terms and we speak to each other every once in a while.

Chapter Fifteen

I started going out with Ilya some months after I finished with Sasha. Our relationship developed from a friendship. He was my dance partner and although he was 19, a year younger than me, he was the perfect height for pas de deux.

We got on very well, but it wasn't love at first sight. We were so familiar with each other that we became good friends at first. He was very attractive though and took good care of me. He lived with his parents close to my hostel and he used to walk me home.

I had settled into Russian life. I had made progress in the company and I got more and more parts in various ballets. But as I started to perform more solo roles, I suffered more with my nerves. When I danced in the corps de ballet I had the security of the other girls around me, but dancing on my own was something I found hard to get used to.

In particular, I found the adagio from *Swan Lake* excruciating when I first learnt it. Though I was able to perform it without any problems, stage fright would usually take over by the end of each performance. I would feel like I was going to throw up and I'd bite my tongue in an attempt to control myself. It took me a few years to get over this. Now I'm at the stage where I could be dragged out of bed and told to dance any part from *Swan Lake* and I'd be able to do it without a second thought.

The only piece that still has the ability to make me sick is *Snowflakes* from *The Nutcracker*, because it is so physically demanding. Sometimes I wish the audience could see into the wings before and after a performance of this dance; I have no doubt they would look at ballet differently.

There are four people in each wing and each of them wears a white wig and white tutu; they are the snowflakes. When the music starts, the girls frantically bless themselves and use a variety of breathing techniques to mentally prepare for this demanding dance. It is a technically difficult piece, but it is not the technique that concerns the snowflakes. The difficulty is trying to pace yourself for what is the equivalent of running a cross-country marathon. It consists of jumping from the wings, starting into a series of dizzying pirouettes that culminate in a continuous circular movement.

The rhythm and pattern of the jumps constantly change, which adds to the breathing difficulties. It starts from nowhere—there is no long build up. Then you have lots of pirouettes while circling around a girl. When doing these turns, all you can see is lots of white heads. When this section is finally over, each snowflake performs a small combination of jumps in an S-shape that lead into the wings. I've seen some people whose legs have just given way when they got to the wings. To top it all off, if the conductor goes too slow, he can drag out the torture for another few minutes. Each dancer has to jump higher to make each jump last longer.

The whole piece lasts about three minutes but it is very intense. All my colleagues hate dancing *Snowflakes*. At one time in my life, it got to the stage where I would make up stories to avoid performing it. I would say that I hurt my foot or something.

All the girls knew I found it so hard because they would see me retching in the wings. My teacher often let me off the hook because she knew I wouldn't turn anything down.

Other days I used to go up to the theatre before *The Nutcracker* and wish I could burn the place down. Most dancers get days like that, where they really don't want to go on stage. We used to talk about it in the changing room. Some of them had considered really drastic steps, like making themselves sick beforehand just so they wouldn't have to do it. One of the girls even said she'd rather walk under a car.

It sounds silly but everyone felt exactly the same. Even now, I would rather do a full four act ballet from start to finish than dance this difficult piece.

One night while dancing *Snowflakes* we had a new conductor who was particularly slow. He dragged everything out, and I really thought I was going to collapse from exhaustion. When it got to the part where we were on the ground leaning forward, we were so unhappy I think even the audience heard us. We were muttering to each other. We were so drained by the end of the first act that we decided to accost him afterwards and demand that he speed up the music for the second act. The girls with shin splints and bad knees were in particular agony. He had slowed the music so much that two of the girls became hysterical because their knees were so bad.

All hell broke loose during the intermission. The conductor had a little room on the ground floor and we went up to his door and started banging on it and shouting.

'If you ever play that slowly again, we are just going to walk off! You and your bloody orchestra can explain to the audience why we've gone home.'

He opened the door gingerly to be attacked by 16 snowflakes. It was around New Year's Eve and we were expected to perform four *Nutcrackers* in a row. We knew we wouldn't be able for it if the music was that slow. We said we wouldn't go back on stage if this ever happened again.

The poor man locked himself into his room, because he was so afraid of us.

Eventually our teacher came down and broke us up, and told us to calm down. The second act was delayed by about 15 minutes because of this. When we returned for Act Two, things had improved. In fact, the music got so fast that we started to giggle. We thought it was better to be too fast than too slow. That particular conductor never really did get it right.

The public often thinks that conductors, orchestras and ballet dancers are so dedicated to their art, that they are immune to outside influences. It is just like any other job, however, and sometimes people want to rush home. I remember one night when Russia were playing France in the qualifiers for the European Championship, *Swan Lake* finished half an hour earlier. The conductor rushed through the score. In fact, when the ballet finished and we were taking our bows, we noticed the orchestra and conductor had already made their exit.

The ballet has only been cancelled twice in my eight years with the company. The first time it was cancelled because the theatre was too cold. It was only eight degrees on the stage, and it has to be above 12 degrees for us to start dancing. The auditorium was freezing and the audience were in their fur coats waiting for the ballet to start. The company brought in some lights and fans to try and heat the place up but it didn't work, so the backstage doctor insisted they cancel the performance.

We were due to perform *Swan Lake*, which is probably the most popular ballet in our repertoire. It is always sold out almost as soon as the tickets go on sale. The audience nearly mugged us because they were so disappointed. Some of them had travelled hundreds of miles to watch us perform. They received alternative tickets, but it meant they wouldn't necessarily be able to see *Swan Lake* when it suited them. It could be two months before we performed it again.

Admittedly, we weren't too concerned about the audience; we were just overjoyed to be going home. I remember leaving through the stage exit when members of the audience accosted us and told us how mean we were to cancel the show. I did feel sorry for them, but it was out of my control.

The second time the ballet was cancelled because of a power failure. By a strange coincidence, we were supposed to be performing *Swan Lake* once again. The power kept shutting off just before we were due to go on stage. We were all dressed up. I was just about to plaster my feet when the lights went out.

It was just dusk, so there was still enough light to see around the room. We were getting quite excited. It was coming up to the half hour call and the lights kept flicking on and off. The lights just wouldn't stay on, so the theatre manager, Anatoly Pitchkalev, came up to the girls' floor. He shouted down the corridor that he regrettably had to cancel the show.

All he could hear in response was a loud cheer. I couldn't see much by now, but I could hear doors slamming as people were running around getting dressed. Everyone took off their make-up and got dressed in record time. We were afraid they'd fix the problem and change their minds. We were due to go on stage at seven o'clock, and in fact they had it all fixed by seven, but all the dancers had left by then. The audience were still in their seats when we left; they were hoping the performance would go ahead, but we were all gone. I'm afraid to say that I didn't feel any guilt. We were like school children who'd been given an unexpected day off.

My parents visited me again in April 1998 and after seeing that my living quarters hadn't improved, they suggested I rent an apartment. I was a lot more confident in dealing with the Russian people now. After two years of living exclusively amongst them, I felt ready to live on my own.

My parents had continued to support me financially and, in fact, if it wasn't for them, I wouldn't have been able to continue with my ballet career in Russia.

I rented a small apartment closer to the theatre and it was a huge step up in the world for me. My parents also helped to decorate the apartment on that trip and they felt more at ease knowing I now had the basics. They bought me a television, washing machine, video, and all the essentials.

I was delighted with myself and to celebrate I bought two Russian hamsters. Russian hamsters are renowned for more vicious than other breeds of hamsters, but I didn't know that at the time. Everything was going well with my new pets, until they learnt how to escape from their cage.

They used to make their way into my bed and frighten me. I would wake up with a hamster walking on my head. Another time they escaped from the apartment and ran wild down the corridor. When I tried to catch them, they bit my hand and drew blood. It was an absolute nightmare.

But they were a great source of entertainment. They were gorgeous looking and I loved them. Then they had babies and ate all of them. After they ate their second litter, I had enough. I couldn't handle them anymore, so I ended up giving them to Elena Kulagina's son.

Then I got a rabbit called Loggy Doggy. I really wanted a dog, but I ended up getting a rabbit, because I thought it wouldn't live as long as a dog and I wasn't making any long-term plans to stay in Russia.

I let her run free around the apartment and she was great company. She was house trained and I'd cuddle her while watching television.

One morning she went into the bedroom and hid under the radiator. I had been at home all day feeling groggy with a headache. When Loggy Doggy wouldn't come out I realised something was disturbing her, so I went around checking the apartment. I discovered I had accidentally bumped against the cooker and switched the gas on, which had permeated through the apartment. I couldn't believe Loggy Doggy had saved my life.

She lost her mind soon after that and gradually tore all the wallpaper off the wall. She also ate all the wires to the television and videos, but I couldn't get rid of her. I owed her my life.

It turns out I'm still in Perm six years later, and so is Loggy Doggy. When I go back to Ireland I just give her to my friends and they bring her to their *dacha* for the summer. She eats the grass which keeps their lawns trimmed. In fact, she's a token lawnmower because in Russia people don't mow their lawns, given that the grass only grows for three months of the year.

Chapter Sixteen

In July 1998 the ballet company went to China. Although I was really excited about going to the Far East, I have to admit that the calamities of the previous tours were at the forefront of my mind. I hoped nothing would go wrong, but alas this was not to be the case.

Disaster struck before we even left Russian soil. The company had organised visas for everyone to enter China. As far as I was concerned, I just had to worry about packing my cases. After I checked my baggage through at Moscow Sheremetyevo-2 Airport, I presented myself at Russian visa control only to discover that I hadn't an exit visa to leave the country.

I had given my passport to the director's secretary at the beginning of the summer but she forgot to get an exit visa for me. None of the Russians needed one, so I slipped through the loop. I had given all my money to one of the girls to mind in her bag and she had already gone through the immigration check-point so there was no way I could get my money from her. In fact, most of the ballet company had passed through immigration, leaving only myself and the artistic director.

I couldn't go back to Perm because all my clothes were on their way to China and I had no money. I was 20 years old and I had never been left in Moscow by myself. In one sense, I had led a very sheltered life in the school, and later in the theatre. We were protected from the outside world, and we were escorted everywhere. The director always sorted out our travel arrangements. At that moment in time, getting back to Perm alone was more daunting than getting out of Moscow. To add to the problems, the company didn't have an understudy to replace me so they couldn't leave me behind.

The airport police insisted I couldn't board the plane without the correct paperwork, but Kyrill suggested to them that it would be better to fix the situation so I could travel. He rang the relevant authorities in the Ministry of Foreign Affairs, and managed to secure an exit visa on the spot. Kyrill had to pay $100 for the privilege.

When we got on the plane Kyrill started to drink vodka and joke that I was the most difficult person in the world to travel with. I was quite shaken after my experience in the Sheremetyevo-2 Airport and I was looking forward to relaxing on the plane. The trip then went from bad to worse. Everyone started smoking on the plane and the air grew heavy. It was disgusting. About three hours into the journey, my lungs were so full of smoke that I started to get sick, as did the other non-smokers. It was a thoroughly unpleasant journey.

I was grey and shaking by the time I stepped off the plane in Beijing.

Although I had managed to leave Russia, I had no way of returning when the tour ended, so the secretary had to obtain the correct visa. This was more problematic than it sounds. We were only staying in Beijing for two days, so I had to get everything organised very quickly, in between performances and rehearsals. On top of that I had to travel between the Russian Embassy and the Irish Embassy, which were on opposite sides of the city.

A car used to pick me up in the morning to take me to the Irish embassy to prove who I was and where I lived. I then had to go from the Irish Embassy to the Russian Embassy to fill out more paperwork. I missed the Russian Embassy on the first day so I had to complete the paperwork on the second day.

When my travel papers were in order, we finally began our tour of China. It was like being in another world. The theatres were huge, and most of them were decorated in marble. There was so much love and attention given to these buildings compared to the other structures surrounding them. They reminded me a little of the Louvre in Paris. They were imperialistic and grand, but everything was extremely high tech. The floors could be spun around or taken off. Some of the theatres had the capacity to seat 7,000 people.

We were very excited to perform on these stages and the amazing thing was that almost all the stages we danced on were like this. There were only one or two that seemed shabby in comparison but even these were far superior to the stages in Ireland and Russia.

But the big stages brought new problems. We had to expand our movements to fill the stage, thus we had to put twice the amount of effort in. Even our expressions were exaggerated to allow for the large audience. I was dancing in the corps de ballet, which was great because I didn't have the pressure of performing a solo part.

However we didn't get much rest while dancing because the Chinese audiences didn't applaud for long. Normally the ballet dancers get a chance to catch their breath during the applause, but the Chinese audience only applauded for about five seconds, which meant that the ballerina had to start dancing again almost immediately.

Hundreds of people in the audience used hunting binoculars, instead of the usual lorgnettes, so it looked as if a pack of wolves was watching us. All we could see was the shine of their binoculars. It was quite eerie. We also had to get used to dancing in the heat and humidity. You could hear the girls in the wings breathing heavily as they tried to catch their breath. The air was so stagnant and moist.

When the ballerina would pirouette, the sweat would fly everywhere, but we didn't mind because everyone was exactly the same. We were wet the whole way through from start to finish.

Even the tutus got wet. In fact, our costumes started to rot because they didn't get a chance to dry out. We would do a show, pack them up and move on while the costumes would still be damp. Sometimes we performed in a venue for four or five nights, but we still had to pack the costumes up at the end of each performance although they were damp.

The costume people eventually started to panic and got a rice vodka spray, which they sprayed on the inside of the costumes to sterilise them. By the time we returned to Perm six weeks later, the costumes all had brown marks down the back where the hooks and eyes had rusted.

Everything that could go wrong, did go wrong. We had brought all our own reels of music to China because it was much cheaper than bringing the orchestra. During one performance of *The Sleeping Beauty*, Elena Kulagina, as Princess Florina was dancing the variation from Bluebird when the music started to slow down; it slowly grinded to a halt. Elena continued to dance as if nothing had happened; the lack of music added a certain flair and poignancy to her expression. She gave a cheeky grin and radiated a confidence which the audience loved. When the variation finished, she took her bow and the curtain came down.

In the background Dubrovin was frantically trying to figure out what had happened to the music. To his dismay, he realised the electronics on the machine had broken.

The only way to rectify it was to manually turn the reels for the remainder of the ballet. Luckily there was only five minutes left, so he managed to keep it at a steady pace 'till the end.

Most people lost weight on the Chinese tour as a result of the tough dancing conditions and poor food. One of our principal dancers, Natasha Moiseeva, lost so much weight that every muscle on her back was visible. Her face sunk and it took her a long time to physically recover. In fact, all the ballet dancers became very muscular because of the heat and the humidity. Our weight dropped and any excess pounds were soon a thing of the past.

The food didn't help matters. We had the same dinner in every hotel, every evening for the entire duration of the tour. Although there was a buffet available to us every night, we only ate rice, tomatoes, and duck, because they were the only recognisable dishes. At the beginning the food was a novelty, but by the sixth week the smell of rice was enough to make my stomach churn. The unprocessed rice smelt like old socks and the chopped tomatoes were served with a thick layer of sugar.

The duck was cut into what seemed to be a hundred pieces, but they only ever gave half a duck to a table of 12. The men in the company got so frustrated because there was never enough meat on the table. They didn't complain much though, because there was always beer supplied with the dinner.

One night Elena Kulagina and I got a little drunk at dinner and decided to be more adventurous in our choice of food. We were the only ones left at the table and we decided that we would try everything in front of us. We agreed to spin the table around and see where it stopped. It stopped at what looked like onion rings but turned out to be snake. The snake didn't taste of anything; it was just a bit rubbery. That night we proceeded to eat frogs and a dog's tongue. It was a kind of blue-black colour. At the time I didn't know what it was, but I remember that it crunched when I bit into it.

We had a great laugh that night, and although I would never eat dog or snake again, I suppose I can say that I have tried them. There was one delicacy that I would not consume. The waiters left bowls of chicken feet on each table, but they still had claws on them. I couldn't bear the thoughts of what they had been running around in; it was enough to upset my stomach. Nobody in the ballet company ever ate them; they were always left behind.

On top of everything else, just days before we were due to leave China, we all got food poisoning. We were staying in a very poor town and they weren't used to dealing with foreign people. They didn't realise we didn't have the same immunity as them. They gave us an orange drink made from unsterile water and we all got really sick. Most of the company had diarrhoea for three days. I was lucky to have a box of Imodium with me. We had a doctor who travelled with us but she couldn't really help. She ran out of supplies in one night. The diarrhoea got out of control. I will always remember people sitting on toilets while getting sick into the bath at the same time.

The hard drinkers in the company were unaffected. Some of them drank a shot of rice vodka before drinking the orange, and that was enough to kill the bugs because it sterilised their stomachs.

The next day we had one of the most dreadful journeys I've ever been on. We travelled for eight hours on a bus that had cockroaches falling out of the ventilation air shafts, but I was really too sick to care too much about them.

The bus collected us from the hotel and brought us to the theatre in order to pack our belongings because all of our costumes had been left out to dry. Some people curled up and went to sleep while others sat back in a daze. The sense of adventure had long since left us and we all just wanted to go home.

When we got to the theatre in question we all needed to go to the toilet so badly that we didn't even make it inside the building; we ran to an outside toilet.

There was a row of toilets outside, but the top of the cubicle only came to my shoulders, but no one cared. It was the strangest sight to see people passing the toilet paper over each partition. I needn't elaborate about the horrendous experience we had because of that stomach bug.

We got back onto the bus and I started to fret knowing that I wasn't going to last without a toilet for eight hours. Kyrill came over and gave me some vodka. He told me to take three big mouthfuls of it and he promised that it would all stop. I didn't really believe him, but I would have tried anything, so I gulped three big mouthfuls. The queasiness and diarrhoea stopped as if by magic.

We returned to Russia at the end of August to what appeared to be a different world. On 17 August 1998

there was a financial crash of mammoth proportions in the Russian economy. The stock markets lost 90% of their value, and ordinary people who had placed their money and trust in the banks lost everything.

Shops closed their doors to the public, because they didn't know how much to charge customers, as they didn't have any idea how much it would cost to replace the goods. It was like Soviet times again. The continuous queueing which had fazed me so much when I first arrived in 1992 was now evident again. People who could afford to were trying to buy food on the black market and paying exorbitant prices for it. The rest were going hungry.

People had lost everything. It was the equivalent of having €1,000 in the bank and the Government saying that your €1,000 is now worth only €1.

We quickly realised we would have no more wages coming to us for a long time. Our company is funded by the state and no government workers were being paid; teachers, doctors, bus drivers all went months without pay.

We ended up not getting paid for about four months. I remember the time vividly. Old people died of starvation because they didn't receive their pensions. The number of people living below the official poverty line rose to nearly 40%, and those just above the official poverty line struggled to survive. Average wages dropped from $160 a month to $55 a month, but the cost of everything remained the same, and some goods increased in price.

By the end of 1998 more than 11.3 million people were jobless. What made the devaluation an especially bitter pill to swallow was the fact that many well-connected insiders had converted their rubles into hard currency, and then got it out of the country. They weren't affected by the crash. There were suicides in ordinary families in Russia—not in the theatre—but the suicide rate rose overall, as did the number of deaths from alcohol poisoning. It was an awful time for Russia; it was appalling to witness.

We were lucky because we had been paid for our Chinese tour in US dollars and at least the dollars retained their value. We could change them into rubles in the banks if we wished, but rubles were no good on the streets.

I ended up lending a lot of my money to my friends from the opera and the orchestra, as they hadn't been on the tour. It meant that I had nothing left for myself. Mam used to send me £10 sterling and wrap it up in tin foil in her letters. There were no facilities in Perm to wire money, and I didn't have a Russian bank account, which was lucky in retrospect, given what happened.

Unfortunately people realised there was money in the letters and I stopped receiving them, so Mam had to stop writing to me.

I was too embarrassed to tell my parents that I had no money because I had loaned it to other people, so I told Mam to stop worrying; I had lots of money left anyway.

In reality I was living on bread. For variety I would fry it in the morning, and then have plain bread in the evening.

I would drink whatever I could muster, whether it was milk, tea or *kefir* (gone-off milk). That was my diet for about two months but I was one of the lucky ones.

Chapter Seventeen

Regina Rogers is a ballet teacher from Galway who wanted to bring ballet to the west of Ireland. She had heard that an Irish girl was part of the troupe in the Perm State Ballet, so she investigated the possibility of bringing the company to perform in Ireland. She thought the Irish audience would respond positively to an Irish ballet dancer and it would be a good marketing angle.

Luck was on Regina's side. At that time the manager of the Town Hall, Michael Diskin, offered to provide a venue for any ballet performances she wished to stage.

They teamed up and both of them came to Perm in 1998 to meet the directors and arrange the details. I met them very briefly while they were over, and I thought no more of it until I was told in class that we'd be travelling to Ireland in October. We prepared *La Sylphide* and a concert programme, which included excerpts from *Romeo and Juliet* amongst others.

The tour would start in the Olympia Theatre in Dublin, and then travel to Cork Opera House and conclude in Galway's Town Hall Theatre. The Russian dancers were all excited at the prospect of coming to Ireland, and it would be a welcome respite from the strenuous economic climate in Russia.

We performed two shows in the Olympia and I was delighted to sleep in my own bed at home again. The next morning we flew to Shannon for the following night's performance in Cork.

I was playing one of the main parts in the *Romeo and Juliet* excerpt called the choreographic organ. Our version is a modern interpretation of the ballet There are four different groups in *Romeo and Juliet*: there are the principal dancers, the choreographic organs, the townspeople, and finally the Montagues and the Capulets. The choreographic organ consists of five couples dancing to a classical piece of music. Technically it's quite difficult because it has a lot of lifts. The townspeople dance on flats and they are the comedy aspect of the ballet. They don't do anything particularly hard.

At the end of the second night, I found a letter from Alan Foley, the artistic director of Cork City Ballet, in my dressing room. As well as being artistic director of CCB, I also learned that he taught ballet on a diploma course. He used to dance with the legendary Joan Denise Moriarty, the founder and artistic director of the now defunct Irish National Ballet. He asked me if we could meet for a drink after the performance, so I agreed. We developed an instant rapport and promised to keep in touch.

Alan and I kept in touch after I returned to Russia. Not long afterwards he invited me back to perform in Cork City Ballet's production of *Ballet Spectacular 1999*, I was delighted. I had to ask Kyrill's permission to fly home for the performances, but he didn't have a problem letting me go. He knew I would be helping to raise the profile of the company in Ireland. I wouldn't receive any wages for the time I was away, but I didn't mind. I was able to survive on little or no money anyway.

Alan treated me extremely well. He paid for my flights, accommodation, and expenses, and when he collected me off the train in Cork, he told me he'd be paying the standard per diem rate, which was £10. I thought I'd only be getting £10 a day, but I was so used to the poor pay in Russia that I thought it was okay. Alan realised I was adding it up in my head.

'You didn't think that's all you're getting, did you?'

'Yeah,' I blushed.

'Don't be silly. The per diems are separate from your wages. You'll be getting wages on top of that.'

He was the first person in the ballet world to pay me properly and treat me with respect. Although he was technically my boss, he treated me as an equal. He brought me around Cork and showed me the Firkin Crane Theatre, where we'd be rehearsing, taking classes, and performing.

I had arrived three weeks before the show began, and we decided to work really hard to get the majority of the preparations done quickly. As soon as we realised it was all going smoothly and we didn't have as many glitches as we had anticipated, we started to relax.

The environment was completely different in comparison to Perm. Everyone was nice and welcoming, and whenever I did something well, they complimented me. This was completely alien to me having spent the previous seven years training under a Russian regime. I started to enjoy ballet and understood how wonderful it could be in different surroundings. This was the start of a great working relationship with Alan, and I've continued working with him ever since.

I learned a few lessons from dancing in Ireland. Although I love dancing in such a relaxed and welcoming environment, I realise that I need more pressure put on me. I had adapted so well to the Russian tuition, that I thrived under its strict conditions and the constant pressure.

Although I am used to dancing with a Russian company, it's very difficult to make a good living being a ballet dancer in Russia. The only way to make real money is by travelling quite a lot. If you have a dancing partner, it's easier to travel and quite a few of the couples in our company often tour. The theatre you work for may not necessarily let you go. We are contractually obliged to do so many shows a year with our company, but Perm is very good and they normally let the people go and do what they want to do.

Management at Perm know the pay isn't great, so if we want to do something on the side, they don't object. The pay is quite low, even for Russia. Most of my Russian girlfriends are married to very wealthy people, so they survive. However, the couples in the company have to do extra shows abroad to bolster their wages.

Some of the male dancers who have cars even run an unofficial taxi service to make ends meet. In Russia there are official taxis, but ordinary people will also stop to pick other people up for a fee. It's pretty safe.

All of the ballet people do nixers because it is practically impossible to survive on the salary alone.

While the experience of dancing in Cork was a welcome diversion, I was brought back to the reality of being a member of a Russian ballet company when we went on tour to Spain.

At the beginning of our 2000 season, we went to Madrid for a day. The organisers had arranged for the prima ballerina of the Bolshoi Ballet, Nadezhda Pavlova, to dance with us.

I believed the tour was well organised as they had chartered a plane specifically for the ballet dancers. All the signs were there. We flew from Perm to Moscow, to pick up the prima ballerina, and then directly to Madrid.

Upon landing we were brought straight to our hotel. So far, so good. We were only spending one night in the hotel, so we checked out the following morning, before attending rehearsal.

That night we performed in the Royal Opera House, which was right across from the Royal Palace. It was absolutely amazing. The theatre seats over 2,500 people and we got a standing ovation from the full house.

The impresario, Tatyana, was a Russian woman who lived in Spain. She came backstage after the performance and hurried us up, telling us that if we didn't make haste we would miss our plane. She paid us our wages in dollars—I received about $100—and left us to our own devices. We assumed we were getting the chartered flight back to Perm at a particular time, so we showered and changed very quickly.

Tatyana put us on a bus and waved us goodbye. We arrived at the airport at about midnight, to discover that we were stranded. There was no plane. Our theatre manager, Antoly, tried to contact Tatyana on her mobile, but it was switched off. We didn't know how long we would have to wait for another plane. All the information and ticket desks were shut, and we were left in Madrid with only American dollars and nowhere to change them.

In other words we were left sitting for eight or nine hours in the airport overnight after we had done our show.

Tatyana had let us go to the airport, rather than pay for another night in a hotel for us.

One of my friends, Elena, was going out with a rich guy and she had a visa card belonging to him, so she bought us food and wine with it. Only for Elena we would have starved.

Our flight left at ten o'clock the next morning and by then, I was so tired I could hardly stand. This plane only went to Moscow; we then had to get a train to Perm.

When we arrived at Moscow train station, there was a bomb scare, so we had to wait about seven hours for the train. We couldn't wait in the train station so we had to drag our luggage around Moscow. We were exhausted at this stage, and I felt the treatment we got was really shoddy. It just wasn't good enough.

When I got home two days after the performance in Madrid, I was so relieved to close the door in my flat and to relax with my pet rabbit.

By the time we went to Germany at the end of the year, I was completely re-energised and ready for another adventure. Our trip didn't start very well, when the train from Perm turned out to be something resembling a cattle wagon. We switched to a decent train in Moscow and travelled to Chernobyl in relative style.

It took two days to get there, and I was relieved to get out and stretch a bit. We had lunch and continued the rest of our journey by bus.

We arrived at the Polish border at about two o'clock, and we all handed our passports to the front of the bus. We were just chatting and having a bit of a laugh, when one of the immigration officers came on to the bus.

'Who is Monica Loughman?'

I was right down the back of the bus wearing a t-shirt and tracksuit bottoms. The t-shirt had the hammer and sickle on it—which was really fashionable at the time; it was the communist symbol. I stood up.

'I am,' I replied in English.

'Do you speak Russian?'

'*Da!*'

He told me to come with him so we disembarked. He asked me what I was doing with this crowd, so I told him.

He went on to explain that the authorities had discovered I didn't have a Belarussian visa, so I had travelled through Belarus illegally. I couldn't leave there without a visa, so they weren't going to let me cross the border into Poland. The young guard was very abrasive with me.

'You are illegally on the border. You can go back and get whatever you want from the bus, but you cannot stay on the border. If you stay here we will have to arrest you.'

I got back on the bus, got my passport, my coat and as much money as I could muster from the people on the bus. I needed money so I could get back to Perm.

We were travelling all the way to Germany just for one show and when I ran into these problems, I decided that they could go on without me because I was only due to be playing a small solo part in *Don Quixote* that someone else could do.

But Dubrovin said I wasn't going back. When the guards had taken the pile of passports and started stamping them, mine was the second last passport in the pile, and luckily, Dubrovin's was underneath mine. They hadn't stamped his yet to let him through, so this meant he could come back into Belarus with me to get the visa, while the bus waited at the border for us.

We had to go back to an army camp on the Belarussian border to get the visa, and we were accompanied back by two guards armed with kalashnikovs. It was about a mile from the bus to the army camp, so we started running.

Dubrovin had some small bags and his coat was coming off. We were both getting hot and bothered.

As we ran to the camp, I said that we should just call this a day—Dubrovin should send me home, but he refused.

We were brought into an office where visas were processed, and the guards there were the most ignorant and obnoxious people I ever had the misfortune to encounter. Admittedly, it was the theatre's fault that I didn't have a visa, because they didn't find out whether I needed one or not.

The guards didn't want to give me a visa, and they proceeded to call me every name under the sun. There was one particular man—I think he was a general of some kind, who kept on calling me a stupid Irish girl. He then continued to use a range of expletives to describe me. I stood there looking at him in shock. I was furious.

'I don't need this shit! I'm going home,' I responded and turned around to leave.

'No, wait. We might be able to help you, but you need to make a deposit of $100 in a bank and get a slip of paper to prove you've done this.'

But it wasn't that simple. I had to pay for the taxis, go to the nearest town, and get my visa photograph taken and be back in an hour before the guards went to lunch.

Miraculously I managed to get it all done and we just about made it back on time. As soon as we got back, the General said that I was a stupid Irish girl and I was too late. He was going to lunch.

At this stage the whole affair had taken more than three hours, and lunch would take another hour. I was cognizant of the other dancers waiting on the bus for us. We waited impatiently in the dusty army camp, while the General dined. When he eventually returned, Dubrovin had to wait outside while I signed some forms.

The General didn't want to give the visa to me, despite the fact I fulfilled his requirements. Instead he continued to call me a stupid Irish girl.

'I have to get out of here,' I insisted. 'I will go to the Irish embassy and cause an incident, and this will cause a stir in Perm as well, if you don't give me the exit visa.'

'You have to be nice to me. Beg me for the visa.'

'Please give me the visa so I can leave this country.'

'Say it nicer.'

'No!'

There was a lot of bullying and this type of conversation went on for some time. Eventually he came straight out with it and said he wanted money. 'If I had money, I'd give it all to you just so I could go. I don't want to be here. Let me go,' I said.

I had been in there for half an hour. If I had £1000 I would have given it to him, just to get out. I was nearly in tears at this stage, because he was a very intimidating man.

Dubrovin kept sticking his head in the door and interrupting, asking if I was ready yet, but this just made the General more angry.

After Dubrovin interrupted for the last time the General lost his temper. 'Get the hell out of my country! Here is your visa.'

I picked it up and ran out the door without even saying thank you, because we had to get back to the border.

After about 20 minutes of cars passing us by, one stopped and gave us a lift to the border where I had to show my visa. By the time I got back to the bus I was shaking. Nobody knew what had happened, and they were worried.

We passed over the border safely and waited to enter Poland. I couldn't stop trembling. Kyrill came up to me with a plastic bottle of vodka. He gave it to me and told me to take as much as I needed. I didn't have a visa to get back in to Belarus again, so we would have to organise that before returning.

I was on the verge of screaming. I took two big gulps of vodka and started to relax a little. When we crossed the Polish border, a Polish man came onto the bus and called out my name once again. All of the Russians went, 'Oh my God. The poor girl.'

The blood drained from my face. He started speaking in Russian to me, asking me what I was doing. When I said I was a ballet dancer, he asked if I could prove it.

'Of course I can,' I responded, wondering what the hell he had in mind.

Dubrovin jumped off the bus in a rage.

'She is a European member so you shouldn't have a problem letting her through.'

'I don't have a problem. I just wanted to know what an Irish girl is doing on a bus full of Russians.'

He left it at that, and as soon as the bus pulled off everyone started cheering. Once we were safely on the road, I explained to everyone what had happened at the Polish border crossing. Dubrovin was delighted that we had sorted everything out, but I would have been just as happy if I had gone home.

We stayed in a hostel in Poland that night, because it had taken about five or six hours to get through the border.

The initial idea was that we would spend three nights on the bus to reach southern Germany.

The only problem with that was a rule that every eight hours the bus had to stop for a period of eight hours. I was taking travel tablets which were making me drowsy so I would sleep for nearly eight hours at a time, which made the journey slightly more bearable. Even at that, it was a nightmare. I would have been far better off to go back to Perm at the Polish border. There was no toilet on the bus, which was also cramped.

Two days later we got to the hotel. We did this journey just to do one performance and then we set off again for Russia. The return journey didn't seem as bad because we knew where we were going. On the way back, I had to go to the bank in Poland to organise a visa back into Belarus and then to the Belarussian Embassy.

The woman serving me was ignorant and rude. She told me that it served me right.

'You Europeans feel that you can come and go as you please, but you won't let us in. You feel that you can just pay $100 and it is okay. I don't know if I am going to issue your visa today.'

I had paid $100 so I told her to give me my visa. She gave it to me after a few more comments.

We were all paranoid that the immigration officers were going to delay us at the border again, regardless of whether I had a visa or not, so we tried to convince the bus driver to smuggle me across. We didn't think we would make it to Moscow in time to catch our connecting train to Perm, which would have been a complete and utter nightmare.

The bus driver could have smuggled me, but he was too scared. Luckily, the guards didn't stop us and we made the train on time. I did that particular trip twice, but I will never do it again. The second time I went, my teacher was in a tight spot so I said I would help out. This time my documents and everything were in order, but it was still a two day trip and I have refused to go ever since. I later concluded that the company were just trying to save money by making us travel over land. The management at Perm don't feel that we are a valuable commodity; we can be replaced.

We only receive three or four dollars a day on those trips and we don't even get paid what we should when we are abroad. We are supposed to receive whatever the per diem payment is for that country, but we don't always receive it.

The company should realise the importance of treating the dancers better. It's very difficult to perform a full ballet after spending three days on a bus.

Kyrill had always wanted to use me to bring the company to Ireland, but when we were eventually invited, he didn't like the fact that I was suddenly the centre of attention.

When we were first invited, he grudgingly gave me solos, and made no pretence that I wouldn't be dancing them once I returned to Perm.

His jibes became nastier as we built up an audience in Ireland, not just towards me, but also towards the Irish public. He claimed they were so uncultured they wouldn't have recognised good ballet from bad ballet anyway. He joked that he should have given me the star role.

To his surprise, I managed every role he threw at me and when I returned to Perm the teachers insisted I was good enough to continue dancing the various roles.

Two weeks before one of the Irish tours, I was walking by Kyrill's office when he called out to me in passing.

'I'm giving you and Ilya *Melody* to dance in Ireland.'

Melody is a concert programme piece that lasts about three and a half minutes. Gluck composed the music and it is a beautiful, but difficult pas de deux. The only people who had previously danced *Melody* in Perm were Dubrovin's wife, Galina, who was also one of Kyrill's close friends, and Igor Shesterikov, who was Elena Kulagina's ex-husband.

I laughed at Kyrill and said, 'How is that going to happen?'

Kyrill knew the chances of Ilya and I successfully preparing this piece in two weeks were slim, and so many other couples had tried to dance this before but failed.

I went to Ilya and told him about the conversation.

'Let's do it, Monica! No problem.'

'I'm scared of heights,' I laughed. 'Kyrill is only trying to make us fail at it.'

As the days passed, nothing else was said about *Melody* and there was no sign of us getting rehearsal time, so we decided to rehearse it by ourselves. We borrowed a video and learnt the moves, because everyone was too busy to help.

The very first lift is called 'the stool', where the girl sits on the man's right-hand, which is fully extended above his head. His left-hand holds her left leg. Ilya was supposed to start the lift from a plié position, but after we failed miserably at the first few attempts, we had an ingenious idea. I climbed up a ladder, sat on his outstretched hand and screamed with laughter. My head was about nine foot from the ground and I wobbled hysterically, trying to maintain my balance. We both collapsed laughing and I grabbed the ladder before attempting it once again.

Our practice continued along these lines for the first few days before we gained our confidence and composure.

Things suddenly started to click and after ten days of practising on our own, Dubrovin took us for a rehearsal.

Dubrovin is a renowned perfectionist and Ilya and I knew it wasn't going to be good enough for him, although it was rock steady and we had perfected the lifts. Galina also came to watch, but she just seemed to undermine everything we did.

'There's no emotion in the dance. There's no connection between the two of you. You could be dancing and talking about your dinner.'

She was right in what she said. We had concentrated so much on getting the technical aspects right, that we had neglected the emotional side, but no one acknowledged that we had achieved what others had failed to do, and we had done so without anyone's help.

The next rehearsal was two hours before we were getting the train to Ireland, and Kyrill came to watch. He asked us to dance it from start to finish. It nearly killed us, but we did it. Kyrill seemed happy with our efforts and said we did 'fine.' We quickly changed, before joining everyone at the train station to leave for Ireland. We flew directly into Shannon from Moscow and danced in the Town Hall in Galway the following evening. *Melody* went brilliantly, and we managed to convey the emotions, while also getting through every lift.

The audiences in Ireland loved the performance and showed they appreciated the difficult pas de deux, in spite of Kyrill's opinion of them.

After the show, we remained on stage while our photographs were taken. Kyrill approached us and congratulated us on a job well done. I was surprised to hear him say that, as I never heard him give praise to any dancer. He began talking about dancing in his youth and how he had done similar lifts in his time. He leaned forward and grabbed me to show me that he still could do a 'stool' lift. Before I knew it I was towering over his head, and then just as quick, crashing towards the ground.

Luckily, Ilya had smelt the whiskey from Kyrill's breath and was waiting for something like this to happen. He lunged forward and managed to break my fall. Kyrill turned on his heels and gave a barely visible shrug of his shoulders as he walked away. He continued his conversation with his friends as if nothing had happened.

For the next performance Kyrill approached Ilya and told him that Igor would be dancing with me in his place, because Igor needed to make some money. We hadn't discussed how much we would receive for the performance, so Ilya took the opportunity to ask. When he heard it would be £8, he just stood there with a blank expression on his face. He simply didn't believe what he had heard. Kyrill said, 'Yes, £8' and walked away.

When Ilya told me about swapping partners I stormed into the green room of the Town Hall, where Kyrill was sitting with Anatoly, our theatre manager. I put £8 on the table in front of them.

'There you go! Give that to Igor, because I'm dancing with Ilya. Igor never even bothered turning up for rehearsals so there's no way I'm dancing with him.'

I turned on my heels before Kyrill had a chance to object and I left the room.

Anatoly saw the funny side and came to me later that evening after the show.

'Ah now, Monica. There was no need for that,' he said, as he gently laughed.

'It worked though, didn't it?'

He put the £8 back in my hand and winked.

Chapter Eighteen

When Regina Rogers asked our artistic director, Kyrill, to bring *Giselle* to Ireland for the 2001 tour, he asked me to dance one of the small solo roles from the second act.

Giselle was the only full ballet on the card, so we were alternating the principal roles every other night to give the ballerinas a rest. We were also doing a concert programme.

My friend Rimma came up to me after Kyrill gave out the roles and suggested I should ask to dance the role of Queen Myrtha. I started to laugh at her.

'You're crazy, Rimma. I'd never be able for that part.'

'No, I know you could do it, if you were given the rehearsal,' Rimma replied. 'Just ask Kyrill and see what he says.'

Rimma had always danced this role and I was concerned I might be treading on her toes.

'That's your role, Rimma. Why would you want me to do it?'

'Monica, I'm going to be retiring soon, and I want someone who deserves the role to get it, rather than someone who is in favour with the directors.'

I went off and started thinking about what Rimma had said. She said it to me every time she saw me for the next four days, and eventually I plucked up enough courage to approach Kyrill.

With trembling hands, I knocked on the door of his office.

'Give me a chance to dance Myrtha,' I came straight to the point.

He started laughing in my face. 'I can't do that, Monica. It's not in my power.'

'You know you can. You're the boss.'

'Okay, I can. But I don't think you're good enough.'

'If you give me the rehearsal time I'll soon be good enough. Give me a chance. That's all I need.'

'Who will rehearse you?'

'Bykova.'

Rimma had asked Bykova if she would train me for the part and Bykova said she would have no problem doing it once I cleared it with Kyrill.

'Okay, then. I'll give you a chance. But I can't give you any rehearsal time. You're going to have to rehearse it on your own time. You can practise on your day off if you want.' I was slightly taken aback by this, as it would benefit the company if I performed well, and by the same reasoning, it would reflect badly on them if I did badly.

'I'll come and watch you dance it in three weeks, and if I don't think you're good enough, then I'll replace you,' Kyrill grumbled.

Despite his reluctance, I left his office with a spring in my step. This was my biggest challenge to date. I knew I was going to find it very hard to fit in rehearsal time. We were performing *Giselle* in Perm in four weeks, before touring Ireland.

I told Bykova what had transpired in Kyrill's office and she reacted with a mixture of delight and astonishment.

'Don't mind him,' she said. 'We'll rehearse during the break.'

The company rehearsed in blocks of 45 minutes with a 15 minute break, so we had three 15 minute slots in which to learn the role.

We started that very day, but 15 minutes perpetually turned into 10 minutes as people came into the room, or the pianist collected her music. Bykova thought it was best to start at Myrtha's entrance, which is a difficult series of bourées. My heart sank when I attempted the entrance because I simply couldn't do it. We tried it for 10 minutes, and then it was time for the rest of the troupe to come back for the remainder of the main rehearsal. During this rehearsal I was dancing the waltz from the first act and the solo from the second act. When we got to our second rehearsal, we skipped Myrtha's entrance and went straight into her solo dance. Initially I did everything wrong: my eyes; my hands; my head were all poised in the wrong direction, and everything below my shoulders was a disaster.

Although everything had gone disastrously wrong, I still had very strong self-belief, so I thought I was mentally prepared for rehearsing with Rimma on our day off. She decided to tackle the arduous entrance on our first day but after 30 gruelling minutes I started to cry. 'I can't do it, Rimma. I'm sorry, but I'll never be ready.'

I saw a different side to Rimma that day. She started shouting at me. 'You can do it, and you have to bloody well do it. Bykova is counting on you. I'm counting on you.'

Her ire had the right effect and I stopped feeling sorry for myself. I threw myself into the rehearsal and by the end of the day I was able to dance the entrance. When I finished I felt as if someone had punched me between the shoulder blades. I stood hunched over, trying to catch my breath. Despite my exhaustion, I was quietly happy that I had broken the first barrier. Rimma was also happy for me.

She knew the role inside out and knew how difficult it was.

I left the theatre that day exhausted, but feeling more focused and determined than ever. Simply being good wasn't good enough. Because I was foreign, I had to be better than my Russian colleagues or they wouldn't accept it. I started taking extra care of myself. I watched what I ate and I lost weight. My fitness level increased. This was my big chance and there was no margin for error: I was going for broke.

I felt I had nothing to lose. If I did it well, it would give me an opportunity to progress in my career; if I couldn't do it, Kyrill's opinion of me wouldn't have changed anyway.

Bykova and I continued to work intensely and after about two weeks of rehearsals it started to come together.

Bykova was correcting my posture and movements less and less. She became enthusiastic and said that I would be able for the part without any problems. She started to extend our rehearsals by fifteen minutes every now and then, so she let everyone else finish after a 30 minute rehearsal, which they were delighted with.

Sometimes one or two of the principal teachers would come to watch me practise. I felt that they tried to intimidate me. They would stand at the piano holding their heads saying, 'She'll never be ready.'

Bykova staunchly defended me and assured them I wouldn't have any problems. After four weeks of preparations I felt that I could dance Myrtha and I would do a good job. Kyrill had kept on eye on my progress, but never followed through with his threat to come and watch me dance. Bykova told him that it was completely unnecessary. Her word was enough.

The big day approached and we performed *Giselle* in Perm without a dress rehearsal. Bykova came to me in the changing room before the show and pressed a bar of chocolate into my hand.

'You'll be brilliant. Have faith in yourself. You will do it perfectly.'

Rimma was dancing a small solo role in the second act, so while the other ballet dancer's started the show, she helped me with my make-up. Myrtha's make-up is more intense and severe than the others. Her eyes and mouth are more defined, while her face is whiter.

I could hear the strains of music from the first act drifting into my changing room, and I was mentally counting down the minutes to my appearance. I was getting slightly unnerved because the hairdresser was still working on my hair ten minutes before the end of the first act.

I wanted to start stretching and warming up. She finished a minute before the music concluded and I ran downstairs to meet the corps on their way back up. The girls rubbed me on the arm as they ran past, 'Break a leg,' they whispered.

I went to the classroom upstairs and gently stretched to warm my muscles and then made my way onto the stage.

Some of the girls avoided me; they wanted to give me space to prepare. I quickly went through the steps, but I didn't warm-up too frantically as I wanted to conserve my energy. I was hoping I would understand the orchestra as sometimes they have little idiosyncrasies and I was determined that everything would go perfectly.

I heard the MC announce the start of the second act on the speaker and I took my place in the back wing. While I waited for the music to begin, I started blessing myself over and over again. I looked into the opposite wing and it suddenly occurred to me that I wasn't Monica; I was Myrtha. There was no room for Monica from now on.

The wings were jammed with people wanting to see my performance: the costume people; the hairdressers; the dancers; the artistic director—anyone who was involved in the ballet turned up to scrutinise me.

I watched the woodcutter dance around the stage, and on cue, I made my entrance with the infamous series of bourées. Everything went perfectly. I didn't make one mistake and I had enough energy to get through the whole act without stress. Once I was on the stage I enjoyed every step. I was Myrtha: powerful and glacial.

When I finished dancing and I was just miming I began to completely relax and thoroughly enjoy myself. All too soon the curtain came down and we exited the stage.

Rimma was crying by the time I got over to her. 'Fabulous!' she whispered to me and continued to weep.

All at once, everyone surrounded me and rubbed me on the back saying how brilliant it was. I threw a big party in my changing room afterwards and everyone's spirits were high. Kyrill came over to me in the midst of everything.

'I haven't seen Myrtha danced like that since my wife danced it 20 years ago. It was brilliant.'

That topped all the praise I received that night because I knew it was genuine. He was married to our former historical teacher in school, Elena Kamenskaya. A lot of the girls said I didn't even look like myself on the stage: my face was completely devoid of expression—it was eerily cold. Apparently I had danced Myrtha in a very old style and it hadn't been danced that way for years.

Ilya recorded the ballet for me and I watched it that evening in my apartment. I cried when I saw myself as Myrtha. I felt such a mixture of disbelief and relief: I couldn't believe it was me. I was so relieved it had gone well.

Kyrill decided I was to dance in the first show as Myrtha. We only arrived in Galway the evening before, so I didn't have time to get any rest beforehand. It went well despite that, and the success and adrenaline from the show in Perm carried me through the first Irish performance.

We continued touring Ireland, until one night midway through the tour, I injured myself. We were in Lisburn and I tripped over a prop that someone had left backstage.

It was impossible to see it in the dark. By the end of the night my knee had swollen to the size of a melon, and I knew I wouldn't be able to dance Myrtha the next evening as planned.

I told Kyrill what had happened and I asked him if I could swap my performance with one of the other Myrthas to give me an extra day's rest. He said that it was too difficult, so he cut me from the rest of the *Giselle* performances except for the last show, which was taking place in Cork. I continued to dance *Melody* in the concert programme, however, as I knew my knee could handle it once I had a break of a day or two. This meant I had almost a week's gap between my performances of Myrtha, and I was very worried. My fitness level wouldn't be the same, and I was also concerned that it wouldn't be as fresh in my mind. When we arrived at Cork Opera House, Rimma and I walked through the whole part on the stage to refresh my mind and body. I felt the familiar surge of panic and bile rise in my throat.

'I don't know if I can do it, Rimma.'

'Of course you can. You've done it perfectly twice now. There's no reason why you won't be brilliant tomorrow evening.'

I went back to the hotel that evening unconvinced and not wanting to experiment with my emotional ability to get through it. I would rather not do it than go on stage feeling unsure.

Show night came around and I was once again standing in the back wing blessing myself. Tonight, however, I felt like Monica. Myrtha had deserted me. All that was left was an emotionally frail Irish girl who wanted to put on her coat and go home.

On cue I made my entrance and floated across the stage.

During this dance all I could think about was walking off the stage, putting my long black coat on over my costume, leaving my hair, make-up and ballet shoes on, and walking back to the hotel. I wanted to lock the door and put a sign up outside. 'Do not disturb! Nervous breakdown!'

I somehow got through the performance though and when I got off the stage Rimma pulled me aside.

'I saw the turmoil in your face. Are you okay?'

I was just glad it was all over. Before we left Ireland I discovered that I was getting paid less than the girls in the corps de ballet. I couldn't believe it. I received €80 for each performance of Myrtha, while the girls in the corps got €40 per performance. But they also received their Russian wage on top of this; the accountant said I couldn't receive my basic wage for tax reasons.

I had to buy presents for Rimma and Bykova because they had been so good to me, and by the time I had done that I was left with almost nothing. I was tired and fed-up and I began to question what it was all about. Was it worth all those years of blood, sweat, and tears in Russia?

Chapter Nineteen

Perm is located at the foot of the Ural Mountains in Eastern Russia and covers a huge area. It is about half the size of France.

Every few years the Perm State Theatre of Ballet and Opera organises a tour of the region. This year the company decided to travel from town to town on a cruiser on the river Kama. The Kama runs through Perm and is one of the longest rivers in Russia.

The tour was part of the drive to bring the culture to ordinary people, and it was funded by the State; so the company didn't have to worry about the finances for a change. We therefore travelled in complete luxury, compared to some of our other tours that I'm still trying to forget about.

We looked upon it as a mini-holiday. The boat was very lavish and even had a sauna on board. There were also cooks on board, so we didn't have to lift a finger or worry about a thing. I was sharing a cabin with another ballet dancer. Ilya had his own compartment, and the opera singers were dotted around us.

Every day we stopped in a different town and put on a show. After each performance, we'd go back on board where we'd eat our fill, relax, drink, and sing karaoke. The food on board was incredible and there was always more than enough for everyone. One particular night after a show I was hungrier than normal, so I ate my fill of kebabs, soup, and salad. I relaxed with some beer afterwards, before moving onto brandy and then wine.

Having lost all my inhibitions about singing in front of the opera singers, I spent the rest of the night singing karaoke. Mind you, I'm sure they didn't consider me a threat when they heard me burst into song.

I went to bed that night completely worn out, thinking I would sleep right through, but I woke up at five in the morning in a cold sweat. I knew I was going to be sick so I ran towards the toilet.

I raced past the bar and into the toilet where I started vomiting everywhere. It was only a short distance between the toilet and the river and it later it occurred to me that I should have gotten sick overboard. I spent the next ten minutes trying to clean up after myself, while constantly retching. I was sick every half an hour for the rest of the night and into the morning.

We had a matinee show at noon and by ten o'clock I had no idea how I was going to get the strength to perform. By this stage I was completely dehydrated and feeling listless. Every time I drank something, it would settle down for two minutes and then come back up again.

Everyone knew that I was really sick. I was due to dance *Melody* with Ilya and the adagio from *Swan Lake,* which is gruelling enough when you are feeling well.

The bus came to bring us to the venue, which was a parochial hall. On the way I was so ill I had to ask the driver to stop the bus for me. Everyone was laughing at me, telling me I shouldn't have drank as much. When we arrived at the venue, I wondered how I was going to get through it. I went to the toilet before going in to change. It was like something that hadn't been cleaned in about 40 years. It was yellow with brown marks. Even the slates on the floor had come up. In Russia they don't put tissue paper down the toilet; they put it into a basket.

I had an adverse reaction to this; by the time I got to the changing room, I had been so sick I could hardly walk. Everyone was still laughing at me, but I just wanted a little sympathy. I felt so sorry for myself, but everyone said it was my own fault. There was no getting away from it; the show had to go on.

Ilya and I were opening the show with *Melody* and the opera singers were in the wings holding buckets for me.

Just before the curtain came up I whispered to him. 'Ilya, if I disappear, I'll be off getting sick but I'll be back and I'll be fine.'

He looked at me with concern, but I needed pragmatism, so I just focused on the dance ahead.

Melody involves a series of lifts, and Ilya has to hold me at the stomach for a lot of them, so it can be hard at the best of times. Then the big lifts started and my face was a picture. I looked like a tortured soul, which was okay because it fit into the ballet; I was supposed to be emotional. When the dance finished he put a scarf over my head and did a final lift, 'the stool'. The opera singers were cheering from the wings, because we had made it to the end.

We were taking the bow when a wave of nausea came over me. My legs were about to give way, so I quickly sidled off the stage, went into the toilet and vomited everywhere.

I sat in the changing room afterwards shaking. I just wanted to put my head into my lap and cry, but I had to do the adagio from *Swan Lake* in the second half of the show. This lasts about eight minutes, and I didn't think I would get through it.

My friend Svetlana made me a cup of black tea and gave me some tablets to ease the cramps in my stomach. I felt a bit better after it, but I still wasn't in good enough shape, so I told Ilya that I wouldn't be able to go back on, because I had just about made it through *Melody*. Ilya told the organiser what was going on, and he got quite upset.

There was no understudy for me, so there was nothing else I could do. I had to dance. I was hoping I would get sick before I went on stage again, because I figured I would feel better for about half an hour afterwards. I said I would dance to see how far I could push myself.

People were saying I was suffering from a hangover from the night before, which made me angry, so I psyched myself up to go back out.

The music started up and everyone gathered in the wings, from the organiser to the bus driver. Even the staff from the parochial hall knew what was going on, and they wanted to see how long this Irish girl could last.

I danced onto the stage en pointe thinking, 'Oh my God! This is so wrong.'

The adagio is quite intense and involves a lot of jumping, splits, pirouettes, and upside down splits. When Ilya put me down my knees buckled. He just gave me a quick squeeze and said that I would be alright.

Towards the end of the adagio the dancer is supposed to spin. I told Ilya we would only do one spin, but we managed to do four. I just don't know how I got through the performance without throwing up.

When we finished I thought I was going to black out but the audience loved it. The opera singers said I was great; I looked so balletic, graceful, and frail. I think I danced the sickness out of me because I was just tired afterwards. I went straight to bed and fell into a blissful sleep.

About three days afterwards we were doing the same show in another town. I asked Ilya if we could change the upside down lift in the *Swan Lake* adagio to an arabesque lift instead. We were so confident and comfortable dancing with each other, that we thought there wouldn't be a problem with it. When we did the arabesque lift, however, I ended up taking the pose wrong and IIya's hand slipped.

My costume was slightly loose and he couldn't get his hands into my ribs. I fell very awkwardly; I ended up being flipped over in the air before I came crashing down. Ilya grabbed me by the tutu to break my fall but in the process he tore off the feathers, which fluttered slowly and gracefully beside me contrasting with my ungainly crash. When I regained my composure, I saw a puddle of feathers by my feet. My tutu was almost completely bald.

I was so shocked and upset that I stood up and gave out to Ilya, even though it wasn't his fault.

'I hate you! I'll never dance with you again.'

We had to perform the same lift immediately afterwards but this time he grabbed me so hard I nearly fainted. He had gotten such a fright that he forgot what he was doing.

I knew that I was okay, but he didn't. He got so distracted that he even forgot to stop me pirouetting, so I started squeezing him and scraping him down his arm to jerk him out of his daze.

By the time we finished we had calmed down. We were brought back for three encores; the audience thought we were great. I think they were wondering how he didn't break me. Ilya was still shaking and I was angry. Everyone had heard me falling, so they ran into the wings and called me towards them saying, 'Come on. Come on, you'll be grand.'

When we eventually got into the wings I went up to Ilya and told him that I hated him

'Just keep away from me. If that has made it onto video, I am never talking to you again.'

'I'm so sorry. Are you okay?' he asked, looking completely desolate. He kept trying to touch my feet to see if I was alright. Dropping someone is one of the worst things a male dancer can do to his partner, so he was upset.

The other dancers crowded around me to see if I was okay. I turned to Ilya again.

'If you find out there was no one videoing it, then I will forgive you.'

He got dressed and started running around to see if anyone had a video. I knew if there were a video recorder it would end up getting broadcast because the fall was so bad. All the audience could see was my bum with feathers flying all over the place.

Once I knew that it hadn't been captured on film, I relaxed and I was able to laugh about it. Everyone was in fits laughing on the boat afterwards. Every opera singer had something to say about it and everyone tried out the position, and then we started on the karaoke.

It was a very relaxing tour overall, believe it or not. We had time to read and relax and I made some good friends amongst the opera singers. A mutual respect grew amongst us and I'm still friends with them to this day.

Chapter Twenty

In April 2002 we toured California and as part of the tour we danced in the Cerritos Center for the Performing Arts in Los Angeles, which is a huge venue.

The Cerritos Center is considered the graveyard of all professional ballet companies, as most receive appalling reviews when they perform there. But we didn't really care. We were just doing our job, and all we could do was our best. If we thought about what reviews we might get, none of us would ever go on stage again.

We did two shows in that venue, and it was Kyrill's job to supervise the backdrops and to indicate to the crew when to change them. Some of the changes are supposed to happen incredibly quickly, so he has to watch carefully.

During the performance of *Romeo and Juliet*, he fell asleep on a director's chair in the wings. He was probably exhausted from screaming at us, and was just overcome.

Kyrill was infamous for his running commentary from the wings. He never stopped issuing instructions to the dancers while they were on stage. We generally try to hush him, or ignore him, but it was only when he fell asleep that we realised how silent he could be. When he slept he looked like someone's docile father. His grey moustache gently moved beneath his snores, and belied the authority he possessed.

When he finally woke up he thought it was hilarious that he had missed three backdrop changes, and just continued as if nothing had happened.

In the same venue the following day, he fell asleep backstage. It must have been something in the air. We had a double bill of *Cinderella* that day, so it was particularly hard on us: we did a matinee and then an evening show.

He fell asleep during the second act of the matinee, while watching us on the television in the green room. When he awoke this time, however, he was in a foul mood. At the end of the show, he came out and screamed at us, telling us it was the worst second act he had seen in his entire life.

We were all aware of his little snooze, so we just wryly grinned at him and ignored his tantrum. He didn't stay in the company long after that. That summer, a motion of no confidence voted Kyrill out. He had been the Artistic Director of Perm State Ballet for 13 years.

He was very good at his job for the first number of years, but he burnt out towards the end of his career. He probably should have left the job when he reached that point. It was a well-known fact that the dancers had been upset with him for a number of years. His lack of commitment and respect, and his rude manner made him difficult to work with.

By the time he finally left, few people were sorry to see him go. There was no farewell party or drinks for him. He left quietly one Friday evening.

David Avdysh took over from Kyrill as artistic director in June 2002. He started his new ballet, *Master and Marguerite*, two days after he joined. He brought all the company into the one room and made us all learn the same thing, which is a waste of time. We spent every other night in the theatre until 10 o'clock learning this ballet and by the time the company broke up for the summer, we were delighted to escape from him.

I was especially looking forward to going home. My sister Eileen was due to have a baby in July and my other sister, Siobhán was getting married that same month. Mam and Dad met me at the airport, as they had done every time for the last 10 years. They were full of chat about the upcoming wedding, and my bridesmaid's dress.

Eileen had to pull out because of her pregnancy, so Siobhán's best friend, Linda, who had visited me in Perm, stepped in to take her place.

Eileen gave birth to my niece, Niamh, on 8th July 2002, the day before my 24th birthday, and she was the most beautiful child I'd ever seen. Mam and Dad were overcome, and it was a wonderful time.

Siobhán's wedding to Adrian later that month was beautiful, and we had a wonderful summer as a family. We really renewed our bonds because of all the emotional events.

It ended too quickly, though, and I was soon heading for Dublin Airport. Mam hadn't been feeling well that summer, but she shook it off because she was so busy. She was diagnosed with pneumonia, and the day I flew out, she felt too ill to come to the airport. I said goodbye to her as she lay in bed.

'I'm sorry, love. I really can't go with you, but please God I'll be as right as rain and I'll collect you from the airport in December.'

'Don't be silly, Mam. You've left me off every single time. I think you're entitled to a break!' I laughed.

I wasn't overly concerned, and I went back to work in good spirits.

When I got back to the theatre, I discovered Avdysh had employed a woman called Natasha Ackmarova as our ballet teacher. She initially taught us three times a week, but after a month she was doing it full-time. I tried to avoid class when she took over. She had come from America and tried to mould us into the American style of dance, but I felt this undermined everything we had learnt.

In the meantime, Avdysh went back to organising *Master and Marguerite* and began allocating roles to certain people. I had returned three days late in September but he had already allocated the roles at this stage. He decided he didn't like me, because he couldn't figure me out.

It started out as subtle bullying. He would ask me to do moves that other people couldn't do. It was a modern, contemporary style, and he was the only person able to do it. We had been classically trained our whole lives. I'd say to him, 'To be honest, I don't really understand what you're trying to show me.' Every time he showed me something, it was different.

After a while I gradually learnt the roles, but when he saw that I could do what he asked, he didn't give me those roles. I made sure to always know my stuff after that, so he couldn't catch me off guard again.

While we were learning *Master and Marguerite*, we couldn't rehearse our classical repertoire because he wouldn't give us enough time. We thought we were going to burst at the seams—we were managing to hold the shows together, but we didn't have enough time to practise them or learn any new roles. We were so exhausted by doing *Master and Marguerite* morning, noon, and night that we were mentally drained and we just wanted to rest when we had the opportunity. It wasn't uncommon to leave the classroom after 11 o'clock at night, having started at nine that morning. A lot of the ballet dancers have children and they simply didn't see them for weeks.

An English impresario called Simon Walton was bringing the Perm company to the Point Theatre, Dublin in December 2002. He remains one of the best in the business, and is very interested in ballet. I was so excited because we had never danced in the Point before. We were doing *Swan Lake* and *Romeo and Juliet*

As the time approached to come to Ireland, Avdysh was told that he had to allocate more time to the company to rehearse for the Irish tour. The teachers realised that we had done very little preparation and they didn't want to let the standards slip. Avdysh focused his annoyance on me. He blamed me for taking time away from *Master and Marguerite* because I was the only Irish person in the class.

During the rehearsal of *Master and Marguerite* he stood up on a bench, and screamed out my name.

'How could you possibly understand communist views? You've never read the book.'

The ballet was about communism, but most of the class hadn't read it. This didn't matter. Like his predecessor he singled me out and made sure that I felt like a foreigner amongst the troupe. This happened almost every day and he made an issue out of everything I did. Avdysh started speaking about me to Ilya in a derogatory manner. It didn't matter that I was also standing in front of him. 'Teach the girl something.'

He was frequently red in the face as he lost his temper so easily. He knew Bykova had great time for me, and took pleasure in bringing me down in front of everyone.

'Your teacher was trying to stick up for you again, telling me how great you are,' he'd say in a surprised tone, while looking me up and down. 'I can't see it myself.'

I never knew how to respond to him. None of the dancers liked him, so at least I felt there was safety in numbers. I wasn't alone in my dislike of him. I learned to tune out when he spoke to me like this, and I'd think of anything but the room I was standing in.

In the midst of all this, I broke up with Ilya. We had gradually grown apart and had become more like friends than boyfriend and girlfriend, though we were able to stay friends and we were both happier apart.

Two weeks before we left for Ireland we still hadn't rehearsed *Swan Lake* or *Romeo and Juliet*. The girls were so tired, that when we finally started rehearsals, people talking, messing, and giving out constantly disrupted the class. They were so over-worked that they had nothing left to give. Everyone needed a break from ballet.

Bykova is very good at getting the class under control, but she wasn't having much success. Three days before we left for Ireland, I tried to express the urgency and importance of this particular trip.

'Come on. We've been working towards this for years. We finally have a big stage, a large audience, and relatively good pay. It's the platform in Ireland we've been waiting for. Let's just do it and stop messing.'

I felt the stress acutely because I knew what a big deal it was to dance in the Point Theatre. I was dancing the pas de trois in Act One of *Swan Lake* and one of the brides in Act Three.

Once we pulled together, we prepared the pieces very quickly and I felt confident and happy getting on the plane. I was delighted to go home, and looking forward to the prospect of dancing in the Point Theatre in my home city of Dublin.

Chapter Twenty-one

I only found out that Mam was dying when I got off the plane. My sister Eileen was at the airport with Dad. It was the first time I had arrived in Dublin Airport to find that Mam wasn't there.

'Mammy is really sick, Monica. You should prepare yourself for seeing her,' Dad hugged me tight.

'Well, let's go now then,' I responded anxiously.

'No, Monica . . . She's really sick, you don't understand,' Eileen said, with tears in her eyes.

Nobody had mentioned the word cancer to me yet, and I struggled to comprehend what was wrong. We hurried back to our house in Santry and I silently prayed all the way home. One of our dancers, Roman Geer, came with us because he was staying in accommodation near my home and Dad said he'd give him a lift there. I asked Dad to go straight home first. I had to see Mam.

As soon as I walked in the door of my home I could feel the heaviness in the air and I lost the feeling in my legs.

There was a smell of Dettol mingled with sickness. I was shaking walking up the stairs and my legs got weak, as I didn't know what to expect.

I walked into Mam's room and, God bless her, she was bloated to twice her normal size. She had no hair on her head; she couldn't sit up and she could barely breathe.

My knees buckled and I clutched the door for support. I wasn't prepared to see her like this. I was either going to pass out or start crying because my mother was dying and nobody had told me. I was looking at her with tears in my eyes but I didn't want to put her under any form of stress, so I blinked them away. I forced my voice to be bright.

'Hiya, Mammy. You look great.'

'I'm so sorry, love,' she said.

'Don't be sorry! What are you sorry for?' I started rabbiting on about dancing in the Point Theatre, just trying to keep things normal. My head was reeling and I literally couldn't take it in. I was completely shell-shocked.

Siobhán was sitting by the bed and I knelt beside Mam and stroked her face as I chatted. She was in horrible pain.

Every time she moved or something touched against her, she moaned gently.

I couldn't keep the pretence up for long because I could feel the tears welling up inside me, so I left the room soon after arriving. I came downstairs to find Roman giving baby Niamh a bottle. I just stood there and looked at him without saying anything for a few minutes.

'My Mammy's dying,' I whispered.

There was an intercom in Mam's bedroom and the receiver was in the sitting room where we stood. I heard Mam say to Siobhán, 'I hope she's okay.' I could hear her struggling to breathe over the intercom, but she was still concerned about my well-being.

The next day Roman and I were dancing the balcony scene from *Romeo and Juliet* on an Irish television show, *The Late Late Show*, to promote the tour. My old friend Regina Rogers collected us that afternoon and brought us to rehearse in the television studios.

'How is your mother?' she gently asked.

'She's dying, Regina . . . I really don't want to do this.'

'You have to do it, Monica.' Regina sounded genuinely upset. 'I'm sorry, but there's no option.'

'I know I have to, but I honestly don't know if I can.'

I started to focus on the dance ahead and the rehearsal went fine, but I felt removed from everyone. There was a buzzing noise in my ear and I felt as if

I was surrounded by cotton wool. Everything seemed surreal. I looked at everyone around me; I did the correct moves, but I couldn't really see anyone or feel my body beneath me.

The day passed in a blur and when I danced on *The Late Late Show* later that night, Mam was sitting up in bed watching it.

During the interview I made sure to specially mention my parents and when the performance was over, I left my costume and make-up on. Roman and I got a taxi as soon as we finished dancing and headed for Santry. Roman continued on to his accommodation and I rushed in the door.

As soon as I walked in the door I heard Mam and Dad cheering. They were watching *The Late Late Show* for the third time, as they had videotaped the live performance.

We broke open a bottle of champagne and everyone celebrated that night. The next day I was interviewed on an afternoon television show, *Open House,* and I thanked my parents for everything they had done to get me this far. I wanted them to know that I was so grateful for all their sacrifices.

Roman and I got a plane to Galway that afternoon where we met the rest of the company.

We danced in the Town Hall Theatre and I got through the performances because my body was trained to perform, but mentally I was by my mother's side in Santry.

Monica Loughman & Jean Harrington

At the end of *Romeo and Juliet*, the music was so beautiful and poignant, that it opened the gates to my soul. As I stood in the wings and listened to the orchestra play the final bars, I started to cry. Once I started, I couldn't stop. The bubble that had protected me from reality over the last few days suddenly burst, and I sat with my head in my hands crying for my mother, who was lying in her bed struggling to breathe. Cancer had greedily consumed her lungs and left nothing for her. There was nothing I could do.

I had finished my performance but I had to go on stage again to take a bow, but I couldn't control my tears. They openly streamed down my face as I bowed, and at that point I didn't really care. I cried until I thought I could cry no more; but even then I couldn't stem the flow of sorrow.

When I got back to Dublin, I tried to get some rest before performing in the Point Theatre. On the morning of the first Point appearance I didn't turn up for ballet class. I had been up most of the night talking to Eileen and listening to Mam's laboured breathing, making sure that she was okay. Regina phoned the house about noon in a tizzy.

'They're doing a photoshoot. You have to be there.' I was half asleep getting into the taxi, but I went straight to the Point Theatre to join Regina for the shoot. Still in a daze I let someone do my hair, while another girl did my make-up. I did a few grand jeté's across the stage, while the photographer took shots. The next day, my photographs made the front page of the *Irish Independent*.

I hardly remember dancing in the Point Theatre that year. I got through the performances in a trance. I didn't feel my body; I just danced. I appreciated the audiences and still felt a flutter of butterflies when the music opened, but all the shows went by in a blur.

The company left Ireland in mid-December to tour Holland. I told Avdysh that I couldn't go with them; I was staying at home to be with my mother. The company had brought an extra dancer with them, so they left me behind without too much of a fuss. I was surprised to see how professional Avdysh became when we reached Ireland. He seemed to realise how significant this particular tour was and he played to the crowds. They left me behind, and I didn't think about ballet again. I had more serious problems to deal with.

I spent every minute of the next two weeks at home, making the most of what I knew would be my last days with my mother. She had good days when she would be able to sit up and chat, and on other occasions she could barely lift her head off the pillow. Dad was like a broken man. I had never seen him at such a loss. He was always in control; he could take charge of a situation and make it better, but when he wasn't sitting by Mam's bed, he wandered around the house with a lost look in his eyes.

My sister Eileen had been keeping things going at home. She took care of Niamh, Dad, and Mam while I was doing the performances, and Siobhán was at work. Eileen managed to maintain some normality. I would not have been able to get through that time without her. I only got about three hours sleep a night, because I was so afraid that Mam would slip away while I slept. When I wasn't by her side, I strained my ears for any unusual sounds on the intercom. Siobhán came by every night and we took turns taking care of Niamh in the midst of all this.

Christmas passed and the routine stayed the same. On St. Stephen's Day, Siobhán came around and told Eileen and I to go out for a few drinks. She said that we needed to get out of the house—she'd sit with Mam and call us if there were any problems.

It turned out to be exactly what I needed. We went to a local pub and I started to relax for the first time in weeks.

Mam got progressively worse after that night and continued to slip in and out of consciousness. On New Year's Eve, we sensed the end was near, and we all spent the entire night by her side. We gently stroked her throughout the night and watched her breathing get more shallow with each hour that passed.

I felt a sense of peace for the first time in weeks, as I knew she was going to a better place. She was leaving behind the body that had failed her, and moving on. I felt a great strength inside me and something guided me to be strong for her, and for everyone else.

'We know you love us, Mammy,' I said. 'Daddy knows you love him; Siobhán knows you love her; Eileen knows you love her. Even Niamh knows you love her. And I will always know how much you've loved me, Mammy. And we all love you so much. We'll be okay. Don't worry about us. You have given us so much love that we'll be okay.'

Dad was openly crying while Siobhán and Eileen looked on teary-eyed. I knelt at the end of the bed and said a few Hail Marys. There was a wonderful sense of calm in the room, and I felt very strongly that there was a presence in the corner. Everything was making sense. Mam was now at ease. She was shedding her frail body and her spirit was soaring. I felt calm as she quietly slipped away at six o'clock on the morning of the 1st January 2003. I felt as if she chose to leave at that point, because she knew it was a battle she couldn't win; she gave in gracefully. She didn't want to drag the illness out any longer, because she knew her body couldn't take any more.

As soon as she died, I didn't want to be around her body anymore. It was a reminder of how it had let her down.

Chapter Twenty-two

Almost as soon as the funeral was over, Eileen had to go back to work, so I stayed at home to look after Niamh and Dad. I couldn't face going back to Perm yet. I needed to be around my family. I found that taking care of baby Niamh gave me a focus and helped me to get on with my life. I didn't go to any ballet classes and I didn't think about ballet much.

Unexpectedly, Alan Foley got in touch to say he was organising *Ballet Spectacular 2003* and wanted to know if I'd be interested in performing. It was exactly what I needed to get back into the swing of things, so I said yes at once.

I went to Cork for the month of March. Our friendship, which was usually very strong, was tested to the core as I was raw with grief and I found it difficult to think about ballet again. Alan had also lost all of his Arts Council funding that year and was questioning the viability of keeping Cork City Ballet going. To his credit, he managed to come up with the money himself, but he was under huge pressure, and concerned about the lack of support and finances. We were unable to support each other during this trying time and we conversed little.

I also had terrible problems getting back into shape; mentally more than physically. After losing Mam I just stopped caring about everything. What had once seemed so important, seemed so trivial now.

Alan asked me to bring Ilya over for the show and I said I'd ask him. When Ilya got off the plane, I was emotionless. He was genuinely concerned when I explained that I was completely drained after my mother's death and I avoided talking to him about anything at all. I simply wasn't strong enough. Ilya seemed to understand my frailty and kept the chit-chat to ballet.

I found it very hard to get through the performances, no matter how hard I tried. I was in a different world, and I couldn't help thinking about the last time I had danced, and it kept bringing the images of Mam dying to the fore.

When I went back to Perm, I was glad I had danced in Cork, as it had broken the fear. Back in Perm everyone was so sympathetic to me, and even Avdysh laid off me. We finally staged his ballet, *Master and Marguerite*, and it wasn't that bad. The fact it had taken a whole year to prepare was the biggest thing that went against it; previously we had prepared full length ballets in a month. Avdysh was in great spirits after its success, and he even let me go home early for the summer.

I returned to Ireland in June and while I was home I got a phone call from the English impresario, Simon Walton.

'Hi Monica. The Russian State Ballet is putting on a show in the National Concert Hall in July. Would you be interested in doing a solo spot for them?'

'Sure, Simon. That sounds great. What did you have in mind?'

He suggested a few variations that he could slot into certain points in the show, but I rejected all of them. The reason for this was because there was no rehearsal space available in Dublin at such short notice. I suggested I could dance *The Dying Swan* as I had just done it with Cork City Ballet. He was delighted and hung up promising he would keep me informed.

This was my first time guesting with another Russian company and the responsibility lay heavily on my shoulders. I was conscious of doing Perm justice with my performance.

It turned out to be a great decision. *RTE News* broadcast footage of my dress rehearsal and it created an air of excitement. When I finally bouréed onto the stage in the second half of the show, the audience started spontaneously applauding and I could hear their whispers, 'That's the Irish girl!'

Luckily my back was to the audience, as I couldn't stop myself from smiling. The following day the papers raved about Galina Stepanenko, the prima ballerina from the Bolshoi Ballet, who had starred in the concert programme.

I made the front cover of the *Irish Independent* magazine, so I was equally delighted. The artistic director of the Russian State Ballet, Vyatcheslav Gordeev, was particularly nice to me after the show. He told me he would be in touch if anything ever came up again.

The summer ended and I prepared to head back to Russia. One cloudy morning while I was still lying in bed, I got a phone call from Simon Walton.

'Hi Monica. How would you feel about dancing *Giselle* in the Point at Christmas with the Russian State Ballet?'

'That sounds great, Simon,' I replied. 'What role do you want me to do?'

'*Giselle!*'

'What?!?' I sat upright in the bed. 'Oh Simon! I don't know if I'd be able for it. I've never done it before. I could dance Myrtha without a thought.'

'I think you'd be great. Will you at least consider it?' he asked, adding that he'd put my name down for Myrtha in the meantime.

I came downstairs and told Dad about the phone call.

'This is your big chance, Monica. You should do it.' I thought about it for a few minutes and then I sat at the phone. I rang Rimma in Russia.

'You'd be well able for that role,' Rimma reassured me.

'You did a beautiful job on Myrtha, and Myrtha is almost as difficult. I'll talk to Bykova and sort it out for you. By the way, it won't be Avdysh you have to clear it with—we have a new artistic director!'

'Really? Who is it?'

'Natasha Ackmarova!'

I couldn't believe that the ballet teacher who had only joined the school the previous year was now the artistic director. I was a little bit aprehensive about returning to yet another new boss.

After hearing Rimma's words of encouragement, I decided to dance the part of Giselle. If I wasn't able for it, I could stick with Queen Myrtha.

I rang Simon back and asked him to give me a month. I would tell him then whether I could do it or not.

I went back to Russia in a great mood and psyched myself up to convince Bykova to train me for the role. She's always so busy that I wasn't sure if she'd have the time. Between classes, rehearsals, and performances, she hardly has time to do anything else.

When I got to Perm, however, I discovered Rimma had already talked her into teaching me, much to my relief.

Bykova said that we weren't guaranteed any time to rehearse it, so as we did with the preparations for Myrtha, we might have to steal time between rehearsals. I convinced her that I would be able for it.

The girls then told me that unbeknownst to us, Avdysh had been treating everyone badly, from the the costume ladies to the conductors, the teachers, and the directors. When his contract had expired, it wasn't renewed. I had to ask Natasha Ackmarova, the new artistic director, for permission to fly to Ireland to perform *Giselle* with the Russian State Ballet.

Despite my initial reservations, she had no problem allowing me to return for the show, and she said I could rehearse for an hour a day, but I wasn't allowed to skip my normal rehearsals in place of this. Although I was relieved that she had given me permission, it meant that I had one hour of ballet class, followed by three hours of rehearsal, followed by another hour of *Giselle* rehearsal.

She tried to make me train under one of the principal teachers, but I said no. I insisted on having Bykova. We had already spoken in our changing room and had a plan of action and she made me promise not to back down.

Bykova approached Ackmarova when she heard her suggestion.

'Don't you understand that she only trusts me? I know how to work her without breaking her.'

They discussed it at length and eventually Ackmarova sanctioned Bykova to go ahead, so we started preparin the variation of the first act. I could do everything in the ballet by day two—it wasn't perfect by any means, but this calmed my teacher down immensely. She thought that if I showed this much potential by day two, the rest of it wouldn't be a problem.

What made the training for *Giselle* especially difficult was that we had intensive rehearsals for *Swan Lake* at the same time. We were getting ready to bring it to the Netherlands and I had to join the company there after performing *Giselle* in Dublin.

We were doing one of the largest *Swan Lake* productions in Europe. We had six lines of eight swans which meant that we had 48 girls on stage most of the time. I was in the corps de ballet and I had a few solos. But it was the corps that was really difficult because there were so many people. We didn't have enough professional dancers so the directors recruited some of the graduating students from the school. This meant hours upon hours of mindnumbing rehearsal repeating the same steps over and over again.

The stage in Amsterdam was huge, so to accommodate our increased corps de ballet, the management in Perm extended our stage into the wings.

We would rehearse for three hours in pointe shoes on the Perm stage with the orchestra. At the end of rehearsal Bykova would clap her hands and everyone would head home.

It was then I would have to put on my Giselle skirt. I was always exhausted and I think that my shoes were two sizes too small by then, because my feet had swollen so much. In a way I was happy to rehearse under these conditions because even though I was tired, I knew that if I could get through this, I could get through anything. It was excruciatingly hard. At times I felt too tired to walk, never mind dance.

I rehearsed it when I was sick and when I was tired. I did it through every different type of emotion. I was coming in to the theatre on my days off to rehearse. On top of all that, they couldn't afford to give me a male partner to rehearse with as everyone was so busy. I asked Ilya but he wasn't able as he had so many other things to do. Giselle dances almost continuously with Albrecht during the second act so it is practically impossible to rehearse without a man. It worked to my advantage, though, because in the end it made me fitter and more able for any mishaps that might happen.

I got the role ready in two months, which by Russian standards is considered very quick. I had already danced every role in *Giselle*, except for the title role and the male parts, so I knew it like the back of my hand, which obviously helped matters.

After working through blood, sweat, and tears for about six weeks, there was suddenly a whole rigmarole about whether I was good enough to dance the principal role in the Point Theatre or not. The main teacher in the Russian State Ballet knew my teacher, and she rang Perm saying that she had doubts about my abilities. I understood her concern but it only seemed to feed the fire of doubt in Perm. This happened about two weeks before I was due to leave for Moscow.

Bykova had to put her whole reputation on the line saying that she didn't have any doubts. She said she took on board their worries but she had no doubts that I would perform to an extremely high standard.

I couldn't believe this was happening. I had worked so hard that my toes were now almost raw.

The ballet scene can be very bitchy, and as soon as you start to progress in your career, there is a queue of people waiting to knock you back. Natasha Ackmarova started giving me a hard time, making snide remarks that I was too good to dance in the corps, now that I was getting ready for *Giselle* in Ireland. Another teacher, Olga Ivanovna, joined in the chorus of criticism and took every opportunity to tell my teacher that I was getting too cocky and too confident.

'She thinks she's too good for us now!'

Olga made me dance on my own in the middle of the floor in front of all my friends, hoping to humiliate me. We rehearsed several ballets at the same time, and

I was preparing George Balanchine's *Concerto Barroco* with seven other girls, but she singled me out when she was in a bad mood. It got to the point where I was sick of her behaviour and I told her exactly what she could do with her *Concerto Barroco*. I curtsied and left the room. It was at this point she spoke to Bykova about me.

However, Bykova didn't react in the manner she expected. 'Monica is an extremely well-mannered girl. There must be a reason for this. I've never had any problems with her.'

All these problems made me more determined to succeed so just before I went to Moscow, I asked some of the dancers that had done the character parts in the ballet, such as Bertha, Bathilde, and Albrecht to rehearse the first act with me.

There's a lot of miming in act one where Giselle 'talks' to the other characters. I had watched the video and put my own script to each gesture, but I still had to put the theory into practise.

A few people had agreed to help me; to show me what music we would mime to, and where I was supposed to be with each bar of music. But only one of the girls who had played Giselle's mother turned up once; nobody else did. I had very little interaction with the mother in the ballet, in fact, and while I was grateful to her, I needed everybody to make it worthwhile. I felt very disappointed and let down. I needed some help and very few people were putting themselves forward to offer their assistance.

At the end of eight gruelling weeks, I picked up my newly-made Giselle costumes, stocked up on pointe shoes for Dublin and Holland and made a promise to Bykova that I would ring her as soon as I got off stage in Dublin. I went off to Moscow with the bare knowledge of the first act in my head and I consulted my notes on the long train journey. This was my first time in Moscow on my own and I struggled to get around with my luggage, but luckily my hotel, the Leningradski was directly across the road from the train station.

The following day I went into the studios and met Gordeev in the hall.

'Monica, welcome! Are you ready for your big role?' I had actually missed the class because I didn't know what time it was at, but I tried to win him over with my confidence.

'Yes, of course,' I laughed. I went straight into a full rehearsal. I recognised some of the dancers from the National Concert Hall, but I had danced alone on stage then. This was my first time dancing with them and I knew I'd be under close observation. That's the way it works when a guest comes into a company.

The rehearsal dragged on and on. It took much longer to get through the rehearsal because the majority of their first act is different to Perm. My dances were all the same with small differences but it is the small differences that can throw you. All the company sat in a circle while I danced; I could hear them whispering and see them nudging each other, but I didn't care. I knew I was doing okay.

It lasted five hours. By the time we finished, I was absolutely exhausted but I thought overall, I had done quite well.

The next day I did a dress rehearsal with Andre Joukov, who was dancing the part of Albrect. This rehearsal lasted about three and a half hours and the teacher wanted to keep going. I knew, however, that I could take no more. This method of teaching was in complete contrast to Bykova's, who knew when to call it a day.

She knew that if I couldn't physically do it, there was no point in pushing me. I always went home and went over the steps in my head. I wouldn't just walk away and forget about what we had done; that is why we were able to prepare the role in two months. This teacher didn't know me so she thought if she kept me in the studio and worked me really hard, we would get more done, but that's not how I work.

The Russian State Ballet was staging two nights of *Giselle* separated by three nights of *The Nutcracker* and

I was dancing the Arabian dance in the latter. I had to learn the Arabian dance immediately after this rehearsal and I didn't know where I would get the energy.

I got to look at the dance once and was then expected to know it sufficiently to partake in a full *Nutcracker* rehearsal. The Arabian dance lasts for three and a half minutes, and it is difficult to remember when you haven't danced it before.

I got through the dress rehearsal by copying the other girl. It was very shaky but my mind was preoccupied with the first night of *Giselle*. I knew I would be fine in *The Nutcracker* and I could always learn it just before the show.

The day of my flight home I had been in rehearsal all morning. I nearly fainted dragging the bags through the busy metro. It was a terrible strain and I was having hot and cold flushes. I could feel the sweat running down my back and I knew then it was a bad idea to take the metro. I hoped I hadn't overdone it; I should be taking more care of myself. I was about to perform the biggest role in my career.

Chapter Twenty-three

I left Russia with the Russian State Ballet's teacher before the rest of the troupe. I had to do a number of interviews with the media to promote the ballet, so we decided to get a head start. Dad was at Dublin Airport waiting to meet me and take me home.

When I got back to my home, Dad handed me the *Sunday Times* and said, 'Read that and see what you think.'

I had done this interview while still in Russia during the period that everyone was doubting me and criticising me. I picked up the newspaper and quickly scanned through the interview. I came across as feisty and defiant and as I read it, I agreed with its contents. I read these paragraphs with particular interest:

Emerging from the corps de ballet for her first significant role, Loughman was cast by her teacher as Queen Myrta [sic] in Adolphe Adam's *Giselle*, immediately raising the hackles of the other dancers.

'Everyone told her she was mad,' says Loughman. 'The company didn't make it easy for me. They wouldn't give me the rehearsal time—I'd grab 15 minutes in between corps rehearsals—and when I turned around and performed it better than anyone else had, it pissed them off. To this day nobody in that company has seen anyone dance it like me. They were delighted as well, but it pissed them off so badly.'

If there is an air of vindication in Loughman's voice, it is not without justification. Landing the role of Giselle is the culmination of a long, hard journey for someone with the looks of an angel and a spine of steel.

'I'll never be a Russian. I'll never be fully accepted by them,' she says. 'I've worked harder than a lot of other people have. If you want it badly enough, you can do it.'

I put the newspaper down and nodded my head. I still felt the same way. It was the first time that I had ever expressed the way I truly felt about my position in the company. I came across as a strong-minded woman and I was happy to be seen that way. I was no longer the timid teenager that left for Russia all those years ago.

I looked up at Dad and said, 'Yeah, that was good.'

He looked surprised.

'But Monica, you can't say those type of things. What about your friends?'

'I can't constantly apologise, Dad. There are going to be 4000 people paying at least €50 to see me. I've put a lot of hard work into this and I'm not going to take it back. I am as good as the Russians so why can't I say that. They can!'

It was okay for the Russians to wax lyrical about their talents but when I started to stand up for myself, people were taken aback.

I was staying at the Burlington Hotel for the duration of the trip. I grabbed my bags and was glad to leave and just be able to concentrate on the difficult dance ahead of me. I wasn't able for a negative atmosphere at the moment.

When I arrived at the hotel, Simon Walton rang. We chatted for a minute and he then expressed concerns about the *Sunday Times* article.

I was completely stunned by his reaction. It seemed as if no one was happy with what I did. I told him that I could stand over everything I said.

'I don't care because everything is true and I'll take responsibility for every word I've said. People are coming to see me the day after tomorrow. What do you want me to do? Apologise? Should I go out onto the stage and say, "I'm sorry!" before I start dancing?'

I was disappointed because I had worked so hard. When Simon sensed I was upset, he told me not to worry and said that everything would be okay.

But I was a bag of nerves. When I hung up the phone I started to cry. In fact, I cried solidly for the next two hours. The following morning I met Simon in the hotel lobby and he brought me to the RTE studio where I was doing an interview on the *Pat Kenny Show* on Radio One. Simon seemed concerned about me, but I was fine once I had rested.

I started to relax and the atmosphere in the studio was upbeat and light-hearted. Pat Kenny knew me so well by now that I felt at ease with him. I started to enjoy the prospect of dancing in *Giselle* for the first time since arriving in Dublin.

The following afternoon I had my final dress rehearsal with the orchestra. Andre talked me through the last minute details and I learnt how to use the props. The stage in the Point Theatre is raked, which means that it slopes gently towards the audience. The Perm stage is perfectly level, so I found this difference disconcerting.

The conductor was very easy to work with. He said that he'd follow my lead, rather than the other way around, which was refreshing.

I had a quick nap after rehearsal, and returned to the Point two hours before the performance. I had a changing room to myself for the first time ever and I was chuffed. It was large and comfortable and I didn't have to put on a show for anyone. I laid out my make-up and cosmetics on my dressing table and put a picture of Niamh and Mam on the mirror.

I checked my costumes to make sure they were okay and laid out all my pointe shoes on the floor. I tried on every single pair to decide which pair I would wear that night. I was rapidly getting through my stock as I had worn out a pair at each rehearsal.

I broke in two pairs before that night's performance. There is an art to preparing pointe shoes for a show. The top of the shoe can't be too soft because you wouldn't be able to turn or balance; if it's too hard it would make too much noise and would be slippy.

As I had done for the last 12 years, I poured some hot water into each shoe, swirled it around and emptied it down the sink. I put them on my bare feet; this is to allow the shoe to mould into the shape of each foot. I put socks over the shoes to keep them clean and wore them like that for about 20 minutes, before putting them on the radiator to dry out; then I did the same with another pair.

I started putting on my make-up and doing my hair; this ritual always calms me down. I feel in control as I go through the steps in my mind. I tied my hair back in a low neat bun and I put blue flowers around my bun, which matched my dress in the first act.

I started bandaging up my toes, paying particular attention to my big toe. I then wrapped the bandage around my entire foot to support it and to stop the bones from spreading. This helps prevent against bunions.

I put on my tights, legwarmers, leggings, warm-up boots, dress and then my coat with a towel wrapped around my neck.

I patted some powder onto my face for the hundredth time and placed it into the bag with my pointe shoes, a cheese grater, a scissors, resin, and a needle and thread.

I was finally ready and I made my way towards the stage. Everyone came over to me and wished me luck: the dancers, the teacher, the conductor and everyone I passed.

I met my Dad, James, Siobhán and her husband, Adrian, at the side of the stage. James was home for Christmas and had come along to support me.

'You look as if you should be milking cows,' Siobhán said, trying to draw my attention away from my nerves. 'I'm only messing; you look lovely. How are you feeling?'

'I'm grand, I just want to get going now.'

I gave Dad a hug and asked him to say a prayer for me. He was as nervous as I was and he didn't really say much. 'You'll be fine, love. Don't worry.'

It was only 15 minutes now before the curtain went up so I said my goodbyes and ran towards the stage.

I sat beside the stage and put the powdered resin in a box and covered the soles and heels of my feet with it, to make sure the shoes wouldn't slip off me. I took out my cheese grater and grated the tip and bottom of the pointe to give me extra grip. I cut off any loose bits of material, stood in the resin box once again and covered the shoes with powder.

I checked the width of each shoe and sewed the v-section on top to ensure they fitted more snugly. I tucked in my ribbons, took a deep breath, and walked onto the stage. I started doing small pliés and a few glissades. I looked like I was in the Antarctic as I was still wearing my coat, leggings, and legwarmers.

The conductor approached me and asked if there was any particular pace I wanted him to keep. I assured him that everything had been perfect during the dress rehearsal.

'Just keep an eye on me, and I'll do my best to keep it consistent,' I told him, and he took his place on the podium.

I could hear the buzz of the audience from behind the curtain and I wiped my cold, sweaty palms on my coat for the hundredth time.

I decided to sit on the floor and stretch, to try to calm down. I wasn't worried so much about the dancing; I was more concerned that I would miss a link to a mime and I wouldn't interact with the other characters. I continued to do the splits and stretch.

Andre came over and once again talked me through the first scene we had. It was evident he was also very nervous.

I could hear the MC telling people to take their seats. The musicians in the orchestra were busy tuning their instruments, and the chatter from the audience began to die down as he announced the leading cast.

'Albrecht—Andre Joukov.

'Giselle—Monica Loughman.'

The crowd gave a big cheer when they heard my name. I wondered why I had been so concerned. They were already behind me.

The orchestra struck up with the opening bars and I ran into the wings where I took off the extra layer of clothes. I was about to peek at the audience from the wings, but I decided against it. I took my place in the wing behind the door of Giselle's house. I blessed myself as I waited, and then blessed myself once more for luck. I continued to bless myself until it got to the point that I had no more time for blessing or praying.

Andre was on stage and it was only then my nerves vanished. I was now Giselle, waiting to open the door to her prince.

When I opened the door I couldn't resist sneaking a look at the audience. The sea of faces threw me for a split second and suddenly I was Monica again. I then realised that I had to do justice to the role of Giselle; my career depended on it.

I quickly pushed that thought away before my nerves took hold of me and I focused on Albrecht.

I enjoyed every minute of the show from then on, and I completely forgot about the audience. I only remembered that people were watching me when I accidentally caught a glimpse of someone I knew in the crowd, 40 minutes into the first act. It brought me back to reality for a split second.

At the end of act one, when Giselle goes mad, she is supposed to stumble across Albrecht's sword, but Andre had thrown it in the wrong place and my carefully choreographed moves had to be adjusted so I could stumble on it. When I walked backwards I hit it perfectly, much to my relief. Giselle died of a broken heart and the curtain came down.

I ran back to my changing room, where there was a hairdresser waiting to do my hair. I flopped into the chair in front of him and tried to catch my breath. Siobhán, Adrian, and Dad then came into the changing room.

'Was it okay?' I asked, knowing it had gone well.

'It was great,' they enthused and started chatting about the show, but I tuned out and left them to talk amongst themselves.

I started talking to the hairdresser, Val, about my hair and what needed to be done. It wasn't long before I heard the last curtain call; I was still sitting in my warm-up clothes watching Val put the last flower in my hair. By the time I struggled into my white dress, the music had already started. I took a second to admire my hair, because there were blue sparkles through it and although the audience mightn't have noticed, it made me feel great. Another layer of powder and off I ran.

The first ten minutes of Act Two went smoothly until the point where I slipped out of Andre's hands in the middle of an arabesque lift. The audience gasped as I fell, but luckily I landed smoothly on two feet facing Andre.

'I'm okay, keep going,' I whispered, and we repeated the same lift without a fault.

Andre was visibly shaken, however, and his movements weren't as smooth as usual. During the pas de deux I could feel him shaking and his musicality was slightly off. His hands weren't in the familiar positions and he had a glazed look in his eye, but I knew it would be okay. I had danced it so many times on my own that I was able to lead him during this shaky period and I let him know I was on his side.

After the grande adagio I ran into the wings and started retching with exhaustion. I had about a minute to pull myself together. When we started taking our bows, I was still going through the steps in my head. I found it hard to switch off.

Through the shouts of 'Bravo' from the audience, I recognised some familiar voices and I couldn't help smiling. I was on a high. The most important night in my career had gone brilliantly and I couldn't wait for more of the same.

Chapter Twenty-four

The following morning I woke up feeling stiff and achy. I felt as if I was getting the flu, even though I had been so careful with my health. I stayed in bed all morning and thought I'd feel better later. I had plenty of Lemsips and I hoped I would recover in time for *The Nutcracker* that night.

We had a dress rehearsal in the Point that afternoon and I tried to remember the Arabian dance, but I was feeling progressively worse and I couldn't stop shivering. The outfit I had to wear consisted of chiffon trousers with a bra-top, so that didn't help matters.

After the rehearsal the teacher hinted that I should remove the top layer of my white Giselle dress as Andre said it was slippy; that was why I fell. I knew Andre hadn't opened his hands enough to support me and this was the reason for the fall, not the dress. I stood there hoping he would admit this because I didn't fancy having to alter my dress, as the costume lady hadn't offered to do it. I thought it was unfair to expect me to do it; I was feeling so ill. They offered me an alternative dress, but it just went past my knee, so it was too short.

I didn't have time to return to the Burlington so I wrapped myself up and fell asleep on the couch in my changing room.

All too soon the show started and I stood in the wings still wearing my duvet jacket and scarf. Despite my heavy clothing, I was shivering and didn't feel warm. I was acutely aware of the fact that I still hadn't learnt my dance, so when the time came to perform, I watched the other girl like a hawk and listened to the instructions that she whispered to me. It was bad enough that I didn't know the moves, but the costume hindered me immensely as I kept getting caught in the chiffon 'bat wings'. At the end of the Arabian dance I felt embarrassed to even be there.

I felt I should just have been home in bed, getting better in time to dance Giselle again. I was due to dance in a matinee performance of *The Nutcracker* the following day but I felt even worse.

After the show I met Regina Rogers who had brought a bus full of ballet students from Galway. I signed autographs and chatted to them. Regina pulled me aside and expressed her concern. She said it was obvious how sick I was.

I thought I would have recovered sufficiently to perform Giselle, but my condition had deteriorated. My immunity had obviously been repressed from the stress of the previous few months. Two hours before the show I asked the teacher if I could remove the variation from the first act. I had seen this done before when the ballerina wasn't on top form.

She refused point blank without even hearing me out. I was stunned. I went back to my dressing room, slammed the door and started to unpick the top layer off my white Giselle dress, while cursing Andre from a height.

I had consistently fought against removing the top layer of the skirt, which is why I was only sewing it now. I was completely stressed out and couldn't think about the performance ahead of me.

I ripped off the skirt and threw it together so that nothing would fall off during the dance but I felt tatty, unlike the glamorous girl that had danced only three nights previously. An hour before the performance the teacher came into my changing room.

'You're not well enough to dance. We've decided to get Maya to do Giselle tonight.'

'But she hasn't even rehearsed it. How can she do it at such short notice?'

'She's danced it before. She'll be grand. It's not your problem.' I sat there thinking, 'That's just not good enough. It's not fair on the audience, Maya isn't ready.'

'No, I'm going to do it. I'm fine,' I said coldly. 'And I'll do the variation as well, if that's what makes you happy.'

She started rubbing my arm and said in a sickly sweet voice, 'You know we think the world of you. We're just worried about you.'

I had to restrain myself from pushing her away. 'Just get out and leave me alone,' I thought, but I didn't say a word.

By the time she left, I was so riled up that I was ready to dance four *Giselles* in a row. I completed my pre-show rituals and stormed out towards the stage. Simon Walton stopped me in my tracks.

'Now Monica, if you can't go on, just say it now. There's nothing wrong in saying you can't do it. They have a backup.'

'I can do it, Simon. And by the way, the back-up hasn't even rehearsed!'

'Okay, if you're not good enough in the first act, we'll make an announcement and put Maya in the second act.'

'Fine!' I retorted, and stormed my way into the wings. Five minutes before the curtain went up, I realised there was no going back and I started to have palpitations. I couldn't feel my legs and the adrenaline was starting to wear off. I started to feel sorry for myself and just when I was about to wallow in self-pity, I snapped out of it. I realised that I wouldn't get past the variation with that attitude, so I took a few deep breaths and focused on what I had to do. I took it step by step. Alan Foley had come up from Cork and, along with Dad and Eileen, I felt that I had extra support in the audience. I got through the first act without any visible differences, but I felt shaky and weak throughout. There were no problems, however, until I ran off the stage, straight into a light that had been left in the shadowed area of the wings.

There was an audible bang that even the audience heard; I could hear them whisper.

Blood started to trickle down my tights and I nearly screamed in temper. I couldn't believe that someone had been so stupid to leave it there. It was an accident waiting to happen and as luck would have it, it happened to me! I was ranting and raving so badly that the backstage crew disappeared. Nobody wanted to take the blame.

The backdrop was moved a few feet back from where it had been originally, so I had no room to run directly behind it. I had to run down the steps, all the way around the back of the stage, and up the steps on the other side, in less than one minute, to make my appearance from the other side of the stage.

I was already exhausted from what was normally a strenuous performance, but this was truly incredible.

I was still seething during the bows and it was lucky I never found out who left the light there. I said a brief goodbye to the Russian dancers, but I was feeling too bad to celebrate with them.

I had a quick drink with Simon and Dad after the show, and I was delighted it was over. I couldn't believe I had gotten through it all. It was only days later that I was grateful I had practised through fatigue and sickness, because it meant I had the stamina to get through this show.

People are often surprised at how little I earn from dancing, but it is a career I love; I don't do it for the money, although obviously I need to make a living. I always thought that ballet dancers who headlined a show got well paid, however, this is not always the case.

I hadn't signed a contract before doing *Giselle*, so I didn't know how much I would receive. Simon Walton rang me two days after the show finished and said he was going back to London, but he would leave my fee in his friend's house. When I saw that it was only $1000, and this included my expenses in Moscow, I left it behind. I didn't want to accept it. After paying my teacher and settling my hotel bill from Moscow, I would have been left in debt.

I decided not to contact Simon about it and I flew straight to Amsterdam to join the Perm ballet troupe. Everyone was delighted to see me and hear news of how *Giselle* had gone. Even Ackmarova congratulated me.

On the opening night of *Swan Lake* Simon turned up. He was in discussions with the directors of Perm about bringing the company to Ireland. I avoided him because our business was concluded as far I as was concerned. The next morning he rang me in my hotel room. He told me he was in the lobby and he wanted to talk to me. On the way down in the lift I planned what I wanted to say, but inevitably, when I sat in front of him words failed me.

He asked me why I didn't take the money.

'It just wasn't enough,' I said. 'I believe Andre got paid more than I did.'

We talked for ages and I was completely honest with him.

'Art for art's sake isn't enough for me anymore. If this is ballet, I'm going to end up hating it. I need to make a living.'

I told him I had to pay my teacher, pay for my costumes, and I had invested two months of my life into this performance. He accepted my point of view and then increased the fee to $1500.

I accepted the money because it allowed me to pay my teacher for all her hard work, so I signed a receipt and said goodbye. However, by the time I paid my teacher and cleared my *Giselle* debts I was left with €80.

I've continued to work with Simon, and now we understand each other's position. He has paid me very well for every show since *Giselle*, and we have a great working relationship. He has played a very positive role in highlighting and promoting ballet in Ireland.

Chapter Twenty-five

The Golden Mask Awards is a prestigious ceremony that takes place in Moscow every spring. All the major performing arts companies battle it out for an award in the major categories: best production, best choreography, best troupe, best solo artist, and so on.

Perm Opera won this award before and our ballet company entered for the first time in April 2004. Bykova told us that she saw no reason why we shouldn't win. We were as good as any of the Russian ballet companies.

We rehearsed *Ballet Imperial*, which is a Balanchine ballet. George Balanchine is regarded as one of the greatest choreographers in the world of ballet. He founded the New York City Ballet (NYCB) and after his death, the directors set up a trust to ensure his ballets continue to strictly adhere to his original choreography. Perm State Ballet is given a new Balanchine ballet about once a year. The Balanchine Trust sends teachers from NYCB to Perm to set a ballet. Perm State Ballet gets a contract for a particular piece for a year. The Trust sends someone back a year later to check if the performance still adheres to the strict production standards. If not, it's within their rights to remove it from our repertoire. This rule stops individual teachers putting their own stamp on Balanchine's work; it preserves Balanchine's original choreography.

It's always a very difficult, but interesting time. A man called Bart Cook usually flies in to teach the corps. He rapidly issues instructions to us, which I can obviously understand perfectly. The Russian translator, however, has difficulty translating the ballet terminology, so when Bart is finished talking, everyone looks at me to see what to do.

I end up translating after the translator has spoken, and we try to get on with rehearsing the show. One of the major differences between NYCB and Perm State Ballet is the way the Americans count the tempo. NYCB can switch between 4s, 6s, or 8s, while the Russians religiously stick to 8s. This causes some confusion, and it takes some time to understand each other.

This isn't the only difference, however. Bart gets frustrated with how difficult it is to get things done on time in our company; it's difficult to get lighting, backdrops, and the correct material for costumes. I feel sorry for him because he seems to be under so much pressure. Everything is always last minute in our company and I think the Americans find that hard to deal with.

We're so used to it that we can take it in our stride most of the time.

We performed *Ballet Imperial* in Perm and everyone loved it, so the directors thought this would have a strong chance in the Golden Mask Awards.

Before we left, Dubrovin told us it would be a fun and pleasant trip and we could rest on the train. I was looking forward to this, but the reality was very different. When we arrived at the train station, I was given a ticket for the filthiest carriage—it was open plan and we were mixed with strangers. It was like a four sleeper with no door; directly opposite there was a two sleeper, but we ended up sleeping opposite strange men. They tried to be friendly at the beginning, but as the journey passed and the vodka flowed they became more aggressive.

During the journey I watched a film on my mini DVD player with some of the girls, but these men kept threatening to take it from us; they intimidated us.

Dubrovin, the principal dancers, and the conductor all had private carriages at the other end of the train. They didn't have to tolerate the conditions that we did. When I eventually got fed up of being harassed by my travelling companions, I got up, packed my bags and went up to Dubrovin. I gave him hell.

'In two hours we get to Gorky. I'm getting off, turning around, and going home. If you cannot provide me with a clean and safe environment to get to Moscow to perform, then I'm not going. It is no bother to me; I have $200 in my bag. I'll just turn around and go home first class.' Dubrovin told me to calm down. He went up and tried to sort these guys out, but it made no difference. They just ignored him. Two of the girls were worried they would be seen as difficult, so they said they were fine where they were. After Dubrovin tried to talk to these guys, they became even more aggressive and the atmosphere was completely untenable.

Dubrovin asked the ticket inspector if there were any other spaces available on the train. Eventually he found two spaces together in a private compartment and one in a different open plan carriage, so Tanya and myself took the private compartment. Elena Filatova was left with the men in the open plan carriage, but she was too scared to say anything. I told Dubrovin to get her out of there and put her somewhere safe, so he did. Elena is married to a wealthy man, as are a lot of the dancers in the company, so she isn't financially dependent on the theatre; she's just so used to being treated in this manner that she—like many of the others—doesn't question it.

Some of the guys from our company ended up getting drunk and having a party with these men, so no one in that wagon got any sleep. By the time we arrived in Moscow, most of the company were dishevelled and exhausted. We didn't feel up to participating in the awards and our spirits were dampened.

Ballerina

When we arrived at the hotel, we caught a glimpse of our artistic director, Ackmarova, who had flown in to Moscow that morning. The fact that she had travelled in such comfort while we were subjected to abuse only heightened our sense of annoyance.

The hotel was very basic. There was brown wallpaper and no carpet, so if you walked in your bare feet you got splinters. There were no hangers in the wardrobes and the towels were the size of a face cloth. It was going to be refurbished after we left, so we figured it must have been the cheapest place available. We just laughed about it and we were so happy to get into a shower that we didn't care where we were. We went to McDonalds, which is always the first place I go when I get to Moscow, and then we went shopping for some ballet things because there is no ballet shop in Perm; we always stock up when we get to Moscow.

When all that was done, we rehearsed until about 10 o'clock. The stage floor was in a dreadful condition. There were big holes in the floor, but they were hidden by a layer of linoleum, so we weren't too sure where they were. It was impossible to avoid them.

We told the artistic director that someone was going to get seriously hurt dancing on this floor, so she just told us to familiarise ourselves with the stage, but to take it easy. There was no way we were able to take it easy considering we had the competition the following day, so we just crossed our fingers.

When we finished we discovered there was only one shower between 18 girls, so we went back to the hotel to shower before bed.

Elena and I were sharing a room. She was ready before me and was starving, so she said she'd go out and bring something back for the both of us.

I was just getting undressed when I got the smell of smoke. I opened the door and was overwhelmed by foulsmelling blue smoke. People were shouting and running past the door and there was a sense of terror. I rang Elena immediately on her mobile.

'Get back here now. The hotel is on fire!'

With trembling hands I threw all my possessions back into my suitcase, put on some clothes, and started to pack Elena's case. She burst into the room in a fluster. As soon as she opened the door, the room filled up with smoke. 'Calm down,' I said. 'It's okay. Just make sure you have your passport.'

She grabbed her bags, and we opened the door again. I could only see an arms length ahead of me and I was choking on the smoke.

The hall was chaotic. Everyone was running back to their rooms trying to save their passports and valuables. Elena stood by the lift with some of the other dancers.

'What are you doing?' I screamed at them. 'You don't use the lift when there's a fire!'

They followed me down the stairs, struggling with their suitcases. People were still brushing past us as we left, although the fire was getting worse. I tried to stop them, and some of them turned around and came back down with us.

We gathered in the lobby and watched the firemen run up the stairs with their masks and axes. Once everyone was safe we felt comfortable enough to start joking about it.

'I wish I left my ballet gear in my room,' I jested, 'then I wouldn't have to dance tomorrow!'

'Yeah,' one of the lads agreed. 'My jockstrap is on the radiator. I bet that's what started the fire . . .'

The thoughts of the firemen finding jockstraps and ballet paraphernalia lying around our rooms had us shaking with laughter.

It took two hours for the fire to be put out and we just sat around on couches waiting for the all clear. The fire had started on our floor, but the hotel management considered it safe to return to our rooms, despite the lingering acrid smell of smoke.

The manager asked us to check our bedrooms and see if we'd be able to sleep there for the remainder of the night. It was already one o'clock in the morning and most people would have slept anywhere because they were so tired.

As soon as I walked onto our floor, the smoke started burning my eyes. There was no way I was staying there for a minute longer, so I went down to Dubrovin in the lobby.

'I am not staying in that room. This building is full of asbestos and anyone would be mad to sleep here after that fire.'

Most of the others had already gone to bed, however, and just a handful of us remained. Dubrovin said it would be almost impossible to relocate us at this hour, but I stood firm. As the night drew on, most people went back to their rooms, until only Elena and I were left. Dubrovin just stood there scratching his head, while the tour organiser, Livinkov, looked on.

Everyone had deserted Dubrovin. Ackmarova, the artistic director, was fast asleep in a different hotel, oblivious to the fire. He was left to pick up the pieces and I couldn't help feeling sorry for him, but I wasn't going to back down. He was getting very agitated with me and Livinkov told me to stop causing problems for everyone.

'Put me up somewhere else because I am not going to die of lung poisoning. If you don't, I'm going back to Perm. You couldn't provide me with a safe journey down and you can't provide me with a safe hotel. If I wake up tomorrow morning and I can't breathe properly then I am not going to dance. Not only that, but I probably won't be dancing for a long time. This is simply not good enough for just four dollars a day. You must be joking!'

'Don't be ridiculous. You're overreacting. Just go to bed, for goodness' sake!' Livinkov said.

'I'll tell you what. You can wear my dress and dance instead of me. I have enough money to fly home and that's what I'm going to do. If that happens, you'll have some explaining to do!' I retorted.

Elena started to cry. She was so exhausted that she just wanted to go back to the smoky room. I then lost my temper with her.

'Will you stand up for yourself for once? If you don't do it, no one will. That's why they walk all over us.' She just looked at the floor, and I continued. 'Elena, you're always talking about standing up for yourself and making a difference. Now's your chance. If you want to go up to the room you can, but if I have to sleep on the couch in protest I will, and I'll go home tomorrow morning.'

Dubrovin managed to get in touch with the organisers of the Golden Mask Awards, and they told him to send us to Hotel Russia for the rest of the night.

It was about half past three in the morning by the time we got there, but we were over the moon. We jumped on the beds until four in the morning, laughing at how well we'd done, despite the fact it took about three hours of arguing to get there. It was a lovely hotel, directly opposite Red Square, and we had a great sleep.

The following morning we returned to the other hotel to meet up with the rest of the troupe. They were grey and everyone was complaining of a headache. When they heard where Elena and I had stayed, they were so jealous.

Unbeknownst to us, two other girls, Tanya Migushova and Lena Levina, had also stayed in Hotel Russia. They just left after the fire and paid for themselves. They didn't even bother arguing about it.

When it was time to perform in front of the committee that night, we weren't too hopeful about our chances. We were competing against a number of reputable companies, including the Bolshoi Ballet, who were dancing in their own theatre. They didn't have to travel, and presumably had a decent night's sleep.

Despite everything, we did exceptionally well, but I hurt my knee halfway through the show because I got stuck in a hole. It felt like my kneecap slipped slightly out. I finished that dance and we exited into the wings. I called the doctor to look at it, because my knee had already swollen. She told me to carry on and I'd be alright. Although my knee hurt, I managed to dance on. Our mishaps weren't over yet though. The floor was so slippery that Elena Kulagina, our prima ballerina, slipped and fell flat on her face. She got up and finished her piece regardless.

The audience gasped in horror, but the remainder of the show was electric. No one had anything to lose now, so the dance took over. We were sure we had lost. Elena Kulagina seemed really depressed after it. She hung her head as she took off her make-up and nobody could cheer her up.

We couldn't believe it when we found out a number of weeks later that we had actually won the award in our category. It was only then that Elena felt okay about her fall. We were all absolutely thrilled and it gave a great boost to us all when we needed it. We were the best in our class on the day. I suppose this night was one of the highlights of my career, but there have been many highlights, and I hope there will be many more. Nothing gives me greater satisfaction than when we pull together and put on a fantastic show.

After the calamity with the hotel in Moscow, it was a welcome relief to travel to Ireland, which was Perm State Ballet's next tour. This tour is memorable for the very fact that nothing went wrong! Simon Walton brought us to Ireland to take part in a Summer Ballet Gala in the National Concert Hall, and he looked after us extremely well. We stayed in the Burlington, which was a luxury we hadn't been used to.

I did a lot of promotional interviews and everything went flawlessly for the first time in my career. Things started to look up.

Simon and I took the opportunity to sit down and chat about ballet in Ireland. Although we both love ballet as an art, I have had to become aware of the business side of it.

Because I was so young and impressionable starting my career, I was more interested in succeeding as a ballet dancer, than carving out a viable living. I now realise they're not exclusive: I have to combine the two.

It was for this reason I began looking for a sponsor. The insurance company, Allianz, had expressed an interest in me the last time I was home, and to my delight, they offered me a sponsorship deal.

When I heard its terms my jaw fell to the floor. I couldn't believe it. I was emotional, relieved, and delighted. I felt as if Mam was looking down on me saying, 'Look after this girl.'

You might wonder where the story ends; the truth is, I don't know. I'm only 26-years-old but I sometimes feel as if I've lived three lifetimes. There's my life as a child growing up in Dublin: I had a normal, happy, and privileged upbringing and those memories are a great cushion for me when things get tough.

Then there's my time in school in Perm, where I lived in extremely difficult and trying circumstances. Russia was a troubled country that had just left the Soviet

Union, but my experiences there made me strong. I learned to appreciate everything I had. Knowing that I had the freedom to leave and come home if I chose was a safety net that gave me great comfort.

Then there is my life now: I have had so many experiences and opportunities because of my career as a ballet dancer. All of them—even the difficult ones—have had a positive affect on my life. If I was asked to do it all again, I would, despite the hardships. I consider the theatre my home; the dancers my extended family. The three principal ballerinas in the Perm State Ballet continuously amaze me with their brilliance.

People often ask me what I think of ballet as a career. When they hear stories of three day bus journeys, they wonder why I stick with it. It's simple. I do it because I love it. For me, ballet is a very enjoyable, albeit tough, career. These stories only represent a small portion of the adventures, the laughs, the pains, and the pleasures associated with my life in Russia. The perception is that ballet dancers live in a glamorous world, but as you can see from my story, this often isn't the case.

I help create a fantasy world in which people can escape into. Although my life can be difficult at times, for the two hours that I'm on stage, I become the sylph, the peasant, the swan, or the princess. These characters can jump higher, stand en pointe longer and pirouette faster. I feel invincible during these moments; I get goosebumps. When I walk off stage after these performances I feel a sense of utter satisfaction and happiness, and I know I did the right thing by sticking to ballet. I search for these elusive moments every time I go on stage; they are enough to keep me driven and happy during the more challenging times.

I'm not a doctor and I will never cure cancer, but the ability to help people escape from their problems for a short time is a gift, and I'm grateful for that gift.

Postscript

I first met Monica Loughman in November 1998, when I attended a performance at the Cork Opera House, where she was dancing with the Perm State Ballet, in a production of Prokofiev's *Romeo and Juliet*. Sitting in the theatre watching the show, I spent quite a while trying to ascertain which girl she was on the stage. I don't know why, but I assumed that she was one of the corps de ballet girls, and when I learnt that she was, in fact, one of the soloists, I was very impressed and immediately requested a meeting with her.

We arranged to meet in the bar of the Opera House after the performance, and as I sat there waiting with a colleague of mine, in burst this vivacious, bubbly, and energetic young woman announcing her arrival by almost walking into the door and falling over in a haze of expletives, as she tried unsuccessfully to regain her balance and composure.

I warmed to her immediately, and liked the seemingly benign sense of humour that radiated from her. This was so refreshing in the somewhat restrained and stuffy world of ballet to which I was accustomed.

She seemed completely unaffected by the virtues of being a ballet dancer in one of the world's best ballet companies, and had an easy-going and engaging allure. This inspired me to invite her to come and dance with me in Cork City Ballet's forthcoming production of *Ballet Spectacular 1999*.

In these performances she was to dance the part of a sex slave in the Odalisque Pas de Trois from the sea-faring ballet *Le Corsaire*, together with Greet Boterman, a recent graduate from England's Royal Ballet School, and Jeannette Alexander from the Manx Ballet Company in the Isle of Man. She would also perform the leading role of Odette, in Act Two of the most famous ballet of all—*Swan Lake*—with myself as her Prince.

During these performances, it became apparent that we had a good rapport on stage and that we were a likely and compatible partnership. We danced together many times since then in what appeared to be a successful combination. I had a ballet company, which provided a platform for Monica to dance here in Ireland (alongside guest artists from the Kirov, among others) and I was delighted to have a dancer of her calibre working with Cork City Ballet.

Each subsequent year, Monica returned to perform with the company, including 2003, the year we lost all our Arts Council funding, and the year she lost her mother—Monica Loughman senior (who together with Monica's father, Eddie, had become one of CCB's most ardent and loyal supporters).

Although a sad time, 2003 proved to be a valuable learning experience for all of us, and I think it's fair to say that many life lessons were learnt that year.

In 2004 with Cork having secured the mantle of Capital of Culture for 2005, Cork City Ballet went from strength to strength. I planned our most ambitious programme to date: a triple bill, which was to tour to five cities in Ireland, including Cork, Dublin, Limerick, Tralee, and Galway. This tour featured a mixture of contemporary and classical dance including *Swan Lake* Act Two, with Monica and myself dancing the lead roles.

Both performances at the Cork Opera House were completely sold out, as were the shows in Galway and Tralee. We had featured on *The Late Late Show* before opening night, and it seemed that the public were curious to know more. In the Helix Theatre in Dublin the show was sold out eleven days before we opened.

The papers raved about the performances. Monica's homecoming as a young star was complete . . . and the media sat up and noticed.

The story of Monica's journey has been an inspiration to young dancers in this country, and has helped enormously to re-establish classical ballet as a viable career for many talented students. Her generosity and gregariousness, combined with an honest approach to dancing (she has no hesitation in telling people how lazy she is!) together with her unique ballet training in Russia, are qualities which single her out as one of Ireland's most prolific dancers.

As friends, we have shared many adventures, laughs, long telephone calls between Ireland and Russia, drinks, meals, rehearsals, and performances together. Throughout she has always been a constant aid to Cork City Ballet's development and growth. Her willingness to share her knowledge with children, students, apprentice dancers (I have known her to stay in the studio past midnight coaching) or fellow dancers is rare and admirable.

Often, when I hear her speak of her life in Russia, I marvel at her determination in surviving in one of the most demanding art forms of all—particularly in a country where, for the most part, living conditions bear no resemblance to the luxury that we are accustomed to here in Ireland.

Described by many as the 'Cinderella of the arts', ballet has a difficult enough time maintaining its profile in Ireland.

Nonetheless, Monica Loughman's contribution to raising the profile of this illusive art form has been immeasurable.

—Alan Foley
Artistic Director, Cork City Ballet
October 2004

Tears of Sadness; Tears of Joy

by Edward Loughman, 1994

(Printed in the National Concert Hall programme)

Please wish our boys and girls good luck tonight, because they are high achievers, hard workers, and dedicated. You are going to enjoy an evening of ballet and see the fruits of the labour of a group of Irish and Russian students who are attending a world renowned ballet school. The parents of these children have made a lot of sacrifices to allow them to attain this level in ballet. This is a very important night for both students and parents.

I am sure that you cannot realise the stress and strain, plus the emotional ups and downs associated with a project like this. Each family member feels it. I know—I am an expert, and I am proud to say that I am Monica's dad. Let me show you—through my eyes—the experience of two years.

How did I ever get involved in this project? I have three girls, all of whom attended ballet classes in Dublin and loved it. I brought them to their classes, attended rehearsals, waited patiently outside halls and classrooms, went to concerts, and heard all the cribs and gripes about ballet. I was the driver, the listener, the confidence builder, the shoulder to cry on, the judge and the rewarder.

For twelve years it went on and I thought I knew it all. But in May 1992 I had not anticipated that my Monica would be selected by Madame Sakharova to study so far away—in Russia of all places. My reaction when she came home was a combination of pride, surprise, and sadness. I was proud because of her achievement. I was surprised because she was only 13-years-old. And I was sad because I was going to lose her to a whole world I knew little about.

The great fork in the road of my life had arrived, somewhat prematurely. A decision had to be made. I researched and read all that I could find about Perm and the school. And soon I came to realise that Monica going off to Perm was similar to me going off to live in a hostel in Baldonnel when I joined the Air Corps in 1951. It was her choice—and we as a family (my wife, Monica, plus the other two daughters Siobhán and Eileen) gave her our full support, because we knew she had chosen the path that was least trodden. But ballet is a competitive, hard, lonely, and self-disciplined life—so how will my little 13-year-old girl manage without her mammy to pamper her or her daddy to look after her? But the decision was made.

Time awaits no one, and before I knew it I was standing in Dublin Airport one September morning helping my daughter check onto her flight to Russia on her first leg to Perm.

Excitement and emotion were high as 11 other parents were doing exactly the same. The day was here for 12 youngsters to start a 3,000 mile journey to the heart of Russia in the foothills of the Ural Mountains. The send off was great, though. No tears from Monica—only a few words, 'Don't worry, Mom, you'll be alright.' Did she see her mammy cry or notice that I couldn't even speak properly? Probably not. She was giddy, excited, all anxious to get going. It was her day.

Knowing that I would see her in January, I didn't feel quite so bad as I gave her a last hug at the bottom of the Aeroflot boarding steps. But with a lonely, broken heart, I waved at the plane as it took off for Moscow.

The months rolled past with phone calls, food parcels, parents' meetings. Christmas and New Year came and went, and soon it was January 9—home-coming day. And back we were in Dublin Airport waiting for her arrival. There were so many questions. 'Will she have changed? Has she grown at all?'

But soon it was all over—the cold emptiness was filled; she was in my arms again. My girl was back—still the same Monica. I thanked God as we celebrated Christmas in January as a family unit again.

Photos, small talk, kisses, hugs and soon Monica was ready to go back to Perm again to finish her year. And there we were in Dublin Airport again—saying goodbye again. Tears and lingering hugs were very much in evidence this time—as they now knew what it means to be so far away for so long—and all of the hard work that was ahead. But at least we knew we would see them at Easter. Our parting at the aircraft was different this time—maybe she realised how much she would miss us?

Easter soon came and it was my time to get on that plane to Moscow with my wife. On our one night in Moscow before the train trip to Perm, we went to the Bolshoi, and with a lump in my throat I visualised Monica on the stage in Perm. You see, daddies have dreams as well. Then it was the hussle and hassle of the railway station, as we boarded the train that would take us to Perm—a long 22 hour journey that no one relished. It was a trip not easily forgotten. Put 32 Irish in a carriage, give a nudge, and a party occurs and a bond is made. As Perm came into sight, a Croke Park roar went up from us all. And as the train pulled into the station, we were greeted by our children, each with bunches of flowers for us all. The awkwardness of trying to get off a train amidst tears, kisses, hugs, and screams is a sight to behold. The lump in the throat again—the family together again.

We soon got to know that icy mile of footpaths and potholed roads that lay between the school and the hotel. We did the journey twice a day for five days, which passed in a flash.

But I'll never forget the first night. Monica and Nicola invited us back to their room for tea and cakes. The room was beautiful—walls covered with photos of home and family.

Then they showed us around their school—showed us how they lived and played and worked and studied. They had real pride in their school. I knew I had made the right decision.

We attended all the classes, met all the teachers, and got to know quite a few of the Russian students. There was a notable rapport between them. I was very impressed and liked the very positive attitude of everyone in the school. But time melts like snow, and soon it was the final evening in Perm. It was a fantastic night—a piano recital by the Irish for their parents and teachers. It was great—my Monica playing classical music! What a surprise! But then over those few days— the surprises were many and pleasant.

The farewell party given by the teachers was something else to write about. It was good enough to say it was marvellous.

The speech by Ninel Pidemskaya, the school's Administrative Director, made us all cry. She said, 'Your children are our children. They are lost to you for now, but we will love them and mind them like our own. So you need have no worries.'

And it went on into the night, but singing and dancing at a farewell party does not make a farewell any easier. Before long we were at the train station again for the goodbyes—stealing the last few hugs and kisses while the Russian boys loaded our baggage. Reassuring hugs and kisses—but the pain of goodbyes is deep. I swore I'd never do the trip again.

Time passed quickly before the June arrival and the concerts in Dublin. More parcels, more phone calls, more meetings, and back to the Airport again. The year is complete. Monica is home for the summer. The world is a nice place after all. But will I ever get used to the emotional ups and downs? I swore I'd never go back to Russia again—but sure enough there I was a year later. Never again I say! But maybe . . .

These concerts in Ireland are very important to us, and the audiences have been great. The cheers tell the kids 'keep it up.'

They need the approval of their peers. Monica goes back to Perm again in September—but with real work on the horizon at the end of it. Our dreams will come true.

Tonight I salute my wife and family and the other families and friends who know what it is like and have helped us through it. So, if you see a man standing and clapping with tears in his eyes tonight, you can bet your bottom dollar it will be me—or another dad.

Glossary

Adagio: A dance designed particularly to enable a ballerina, generally assisted by a male partner, to display her grace, sense of line, and perfect balance. Also a generic term for a series of exercises designed to develop grace, sense of line, and balance.

Arabesque: A pose in which the dancer raises one leg, with the knee straight, directly behind the body.

Attitude: A pose in which the dancer raises one leg directly behind the body with the knee bent at a right angle. The knee is then as high as or higher than the foot, and the foot points to the dancer's side.

Ballerina: A principal woman dancer of a ballet company.

Prima Ballerina: The star dancer.

Ballet Blanc, or While Ballet: A ballet in which the dancing is considered purely classical.

Ballon: The ability to hold a pose in the air.

Barre: A wooden pole, usually fixed horizontally to a wall, that dancers hold for support in certain exercises.

Choreographer: A person who composes ballets or other dances.

Corps de Ballet: Those dancers who perform only in the group numbers.

Danseur: A male dancer.

Premier Danseur: The star male dancer.

Danseuse: A female dancer.

Divertissement: A group of short dances inserted in a classical ballet. They usually have little to do with the plot.

Entrechat: A jump in which one foot crosses in front of the other and then behind while the dancer is in the air. Entrechats are numbered from deux to dix (two to ten) according to the number of movements performed, with each crossing of the legs counted as two movements.

Fourette: A turn in which the dancer, standing on one foot, uses the other leg in a circular whip-like motion to pull the body.

Jeté: A jump from one leg to the other.

Grand Jeté: A great jump.

Maitre de Ballet or Ballet Master: A person, generally associated with a specific company, who composes ballets and other dances and who is responsible for the training of dancers and the maintenance of their technique.

Pas: A single step or combination of steps forming a dance.

Pas de Deux: A dance for two persons that in classical ballet has an adagio, in which the male dancer supports the ballerina in slow movements; a solo dance for each; and a coda, or ending, in which the couple dance apart and together with all their technical skill.

Pirouette: A complete turn on one foot, with the swing of an arm providing the force.

Plié: A full bending of the knees in any of the five positions. Ina all positions but second and forth ouverte the heels will come off the ground.

Demi-plié: Half-bending of the knees without raising the heels off the ground at any time.

Port de Bras: A generic term for a group of exercises designed to make the arms move gracefully. The term also refers to any specific movement of the arms.

Tutu: The very short skirt that was first worn by ballerinas in Romantic ballets of the 19th Century.